God Bless

Dr. Bob

Living Up In
A Down World

Living Life Grace " fully"!

Dr. Bob Edwards

iUniverse, Inc.
Bloomington

Living Up In A Down World
Living Life Grace "fully"!

iUniverse books may be ordered through booksellers or by contacting:

iUniverse
1663 Liberty Drive
Bloomington, IN 47403
www.iuniverse.com
1-800-Authors (1-800-288-4677)

Because of the dynamic nature of the Internet, any Web addresses or links contained in this book may have changed since publication and may no longer be valid.

Any people depicted in stock imagery provided by Thinkstock are models, and such images are being used for illustrative purposes only.

Certain stock imagery © Thinkstock.

ISBN: 978-1-4502-7768-6 (sc)
ISBN: 978-1-4502-7770-9 (ebk)

Printed in the United States of America

iUniverse rev. date: 1/20/2011

Contents

Author's Note to the Reader

What is this book about and what will it do for you? Practically speaking, this is a funny book with powerful stories of human nature, all designed to illustrate how we so easily live down in this world given for us to enjoy. In a nutshell, the book gives you a pattern to just live life! We are so empowered by the Father, through a relationship with Christ and grace, that we can literally just live life and live it to the fullest. ***I promise this book will help you live life well.***

I tried to describe in the overview how we have distorted the life-giving Gospel. I believe that we live under a deep sense of shame and guilt that was not the intention of the Creator and the author of the Bible. We have adopted the life given to us by our surroundings and not understood the power to live life in Him. These early chapters are crucial. They lay the foundation for the remainder of the practical answers offered later in the text. The later part of the book is a step by step sharing how to in various subjects.

There is a great deal of humor in the book! Awesome stories have been used of real people, all drawn to give us real answers to the difficult questions of who we are, whose we are, and how we can live up in a down world. I promise a thrilling, non-technical escapade into joy, using humor and witty anecdotes for overcoming anxieties, depression, and other "lesser journeys" we take. God intended us for the greater journey. Now, go forward and enjoy!

Further, this book is a basic introduction to the way to personal peace. I feel the greatest need this generation has is to find and sustain a deep sense of purpose and meaning. We are an empty people; isolated by technology, fear of "religion", and a generation that finds trust difficult to receive or give. By examining the way we think, feel, and process all the "truth" that is around us, we can obtain the gift of graceful living God promised in His scriptures. It is a light hearted, easily followed text, that provides an outline for the path or process to discover and live a lifetime of peace and fulfillment; all of this done as we realize our real spiritual selves. These new revelations empower the privilege of being a Christian disciple in this century. It is to this power and peace we were born.

About the author: I am a native of the South and migrated to the frozen north to direct the Samaritan Center in Minot, North Dakota. I am currently the senior pastor of First Presbyterian Church in Minot. I have twenty nine years in ministry, most of which was spent as a counselor and director of mental health facilities. During this time, I also served as supply pastor in several locations. I have a doctorate in psychology, majoring in counseling. I have my Masters in Divinity and am also a clinical member of the American Association of Marriage and Family Therapist (AAMFT). I speak nationally and have enjoyed a great relationship with audiences for over ten years. I am the President and CEO of Upward Living Ministries. I have five children and two grandchildren.

It is my prayer that you will find this book enjoyable, practical, and life challenging! Shalom!

Dr. Bob Edwards
Websites: www.livingup.org, www.minotfpc.org

Dedication

This book is dedicated to my parents, Dorothy and Bob Edwards, Sr.; to a mom who loved me in a very special way and to a dad who taught me carefully to achieve and go for the best you can do. Thanks!

Also, I wish to thank the people of First Presbyterian Church in Minot, North Dakota for their patience and permission to pursue this adventure. Shalom!

Introduction:
Basic Thoughts and Concepts

There is a story told about a man in the desert who lost his camel. He went about asking people, "Have you seen my camel?" Some just shook their heads while others didn't bother to answer. Some simply ignored him. Finally, he came upon another man and he said, "Have you seen my camel?" To which the man responded, "Did he have a lame foot?" "Yes! Yes, he did have a lame foot." "Well, did he have a tooth missing?" "Yes, yes!" said the man, "you've seen my camel!" "Was he carrying fruits and spices?" "Yes! Yes," said the man, "you've seen my camel, where is my camel?" To which the man replied, "No, I haven't seen your camel, but I have seen evidence that he has been here. I noticed one lighter footprint in the sand and I figured he had a lame foot, which he favored. I noticed tuffs of grass left, and I surmised that he had a missing tooth. And I saw ants and flies along the way and I knew it must be that he was carrying fruits and spices. No I haven't seen your camel, but I have seen evidence that he's been here."

Not everyone will see, or needs to see, the evidence of your acts of kindness; but time spent listening, the gentle pat on the shoulder, a smile, the hand held, the prayers offered, or the errands run do matter. It will make such a difference in someone's life and somehow, somewhere, they will see evidence that we have been there. So our prayer might be this, "We thank you for those who have been there for us, who have taught us. Bless us as we read this book and help us Lord to receive and apply your truth as we find it in these pages. Amen".

I want to thank my friend Ruth Coleman for the above story. She was one of many people that helped me along the way to introduce these ideas for "Making Life Work". *Living Up In A Down World* is about my journey. The story above is about a man whose kindness is often unnoticed, as are the stories and the people described in this book chiefly unnoticed and unaware of the great contribution they made to my life. The stories are drawn from people, all through my life, who have given insight and inspiration, yet often unacknowledged.

The idea for *Living Up In A Down World* was conceived from a speech I presented to the graduating class of a local high school. I worked and labored to bring what I hoped would be something to be remembered, not boring but dynamic. It had to be dynamic because I was following an old friend who was probably one of the best speakers ever, humorous and gifted! His name is Rolf Nestingen, a Lutheran pastor and good friend. I remember feeling like the class enjoyed the talk and for several years thereafter people would comment that they really enjoyed the concepts and expressed that the title of the talk was curious and intriguing. So it is that the idea for a book began and as the interest in my heart increased, I felt encouraged to write more about how to make life work from a practical Christian, down to earth, livable perspective. To this idea then I write this first volume, dedicated to our Lord and given in hopes that the concepts of living up and being at personal peace will bring joy to many hearts.

Where do you start? Living up in a down world, where do you start? Life is often very similar to the diagram you see below.

What do you see? Where do you start? It is quit difficult and complex. With just a little guidance and a hint of direction, what happens? The difficulty is much less if I show you the following maze? The difference is direction, a direction given by someone to help start the journey. The difference is that a direction is introduced, a direction given by someone to help start or mature the journey.

In this diagram, I gave you the starting arrow and added numbers to guide your path. Now every one of us can solve the maze, and rapidly move to the solution. So, where do we begin? We begin by simply getting started. This introduction is intended to be the overview of the next several chapters. It is a synopsis, an overview statement of where the book will be taking our thoughts.

One of the basic premises for this book is that all truth is derived from God's Word and that our worldview can be transformed by God's Word (Romans 12:1-2), that God has provided all that we need for good and healthy living. Another basic premise is that a personal peace, founded in grace, is very possible, and is promised by God to be our inheritance in Christ (John 14:26-27). I believe that the ability to live up in a down world is accomplished by consciously applying biblical principles, using the information of good psychological techniques, and consistently making the attempt to blend the two into one concept for life;. This blending of the worlds of psychology and faith producing a thoroughly biblical and faith based vantage point! I point out this idea because I fear that for many of us, psychotherapy is seen as "psycho-babble" and, thus, we don't ever give the blend of scripture and psychology a chance.

I've practiced psychotherapy for twenty five years. During that time, I have realized certain truths through the inspiration of the Holy Spirit or by the lessons learned in the journey. I call these "revelizations" or realized truths; these are revelations that I have realized and then applied to my life. I believe that many of the techniques or concepts we use to manage our lives are based in what we've learned, what we've then practiced, what we've then applied; and then, as we mature, we hopefully realize what must be challenged or changed in order for growth to happen. In other words, our histories, our upbringing, our learned behaviors, those patterns that we have practiced and learned, will by the very nature become the way that we live our lives. This constellation of thoughts and impressions then forms what is known as our personality.

It follows that if pain or distress continues and the cost of continuing the behavior is too high; we change, or the pain continues. This pain creates in us an inability to process correctly. This "fractured thinking" often produces a number of inappropriate adaptive mindsets, addictions, or self medications solely established by the mind to make the pain go away. For example, overeating, workaholics, alcoholism, rigid legalism, perfectionism, and on and on goes the list of "isms" that affect us.. This is not a statement of blame, or the excuse to blame our current behaviors on our childhood injuries or memories; but rather, is a statement of "vehicle", a part of our total selves that needs to be examined and counteracted by scripture. Our choices are our choices and we are responsible for them, regardless of our histories!

In order for humankind or individuals to change basic personality drives and schemas (the way in which life works for us), insights must be gained and these insights often only occur when the pain is high enough. The New Testament tells us to welcome tribulation because in the process of pain, growth occurs; primarily because of the necessity of leaning into God and not into our own strength (Proverbs 3:5-6). The pain, with time and thought, creates new insights for our matrix or worldview. These insights, then, create the ability to make empowered choices for change. If changes are not made, and new ways to think are not formed, conflict ensues and this conflict often creates within the personality a binding up of our spirit; a place where the grace that was designed to set us free has in fact created a prison of guilt and shame.

I call this "toxic guilt" or the "prison of ought-ness". If we receive the gift of grace and do not or cannot process the shame and the guilt, then what was presented by Christ as a free gift becomes a prison of "ought and should" that ends up presenting to our up world a very down worldview. I will speak more of this in the section on "Barriers to Overcome". For now, let it be enough to say that Jesus was so concerned about legalistic bondage that he chastised and warned the Pharisees, and the new Christian leaders, about leading a convert to the way of Israel/faith, and then binding them up with more to do's than even their forefathers could manage.

Let us be careful at this point to note that obedience is the desire and command of Christ, but it is not, and does not need to become the measure of our salvation or the definer of our personal relationship with Christ. In Christ, the work is complete. The necessity for obedience is certainly called for in the scriptures. This obedience is a rightful response to the overabounding grace of God. We are not "good" when we perform obediently; we are "good" by the actions of the One God gave us! We are good period! Wanting to be called a "good boy who does a good job" is natural. It is a reaction to the joy of grace.

Our obedience is rewarded but it does not secure or deny our salvation, grace does in Christ. Christ said it was finished in him. Where does the ability to live and to be consistent in our obedience begin or end? Where does the works we've done meet the line of salvation through acceptable obedience begin or end; solely at the cross and finished gift of grace. The act of willful obedience is the joy of the child pleasing the Father. Are we guilty of "ought-ness" sometimes? Does the guilt and toxic shame of our histories, combined with the injuries caused by the misinterpretation of our caring parents' actions, create in us a very Down World experience that God fully intended to be an Up World joy! This thought or concept is absolutely true! This need or drive to be loved by our actions, rather than knowing we are loved by His actions, is the very crux of legalistic thinking. We can never measure up because we will always keep moving the goal line!

Let me parenthetically say at this time, this is not a blanket excuse for us to blame our childhoods for where we are today. This want to blame is reminiscent of the garden where Adam and Eve played the pointing game; "She did it, no, the snake did!" It is true our parents often did the very best thing they knew how to do. It is true that in some instances, the parenting was very poor; but for the vast majority of us, God blessed us with hard working, caring, very much trying parents. Our neurotic thinking, if blamed on our childhoods, will go uncorrected and the ever-popular game of blame will freeze our joys of responsible, responsive lives.

It is my belief that life, and the way we think about life, centers around the verse Proverbs 23:7, "As a man thinks in his heart so is he." What we are really doing, in this process of living up in life, is challenging the way that we think and correcting that thinking, and subsequent feelings that follow. How, you might ask? By replacing those "stinking thinkings" with new truths from God's Word; this is the key! This produces a replaced way of looking at the life situation that is in front of you. In this way, we rethink our worldview and organize new ways to process our "believed perceptions". To fail to enter this thought process, or this transformation, is to stagnant and decay our joy to the point that we become depressed. One out of eight people are clinically challenged by depression during their lives. This depressed mood is created primarily because we fear facing the challenges of change. As the Holy Spirit reveals to us "awareness' of our brokenness'", then it is our responsibility to learn, discern, and apply. Remember the basic premise that all truth is from God and that personal peace is possible, in fact, our birthright as the adopted children of God. Living up in a down world is all about believing and receiving; believing what God said (Psalm 91:2) and being able to emotionally receive it (Philippians 2:5 and 4:8).

To make my point, let's hear a quote from James Allen, the author of *As a Man Thinketh*. The aphorism, "as a man thinketh in his heart so is he", not only embraces the whole of the man's being, but is so comprehensive as to reach out to every condition and circumstance of his life. A man is literally what he thinks, his character being the complete sum of all of his thoughts. As the plant springs from and could not be without the seed, so every act of a man springs from the hidden seeds of thought. These thoughts are given by the revelation of the Holy Spirit and true, or these thoughts are influenced by the adversary, believed, then practiced and made true by our own sinful "flesh" nature. This rationale applies equally to those acts called spontaneous and unpremeditated, as well as to those that are deliberately executed. Man is made or unmade by himself in the armory of thought. He forges the weapons by which he destroys himself; he also fashions the tools with which he builds for himself heavenly mansions of joy and strength and peace. By the right choice in true application of thought, man ascends to the Divine Perfection, by the abuse and wrong application of thought, he descends below the level of the beast. Between these two extremes are all the grades of character, and demand is their maker and master. Let's proceed a little further with developing the ABC's of our "destroyed" peace. Remember, the goal is to live a life up in a fallen down world.

For many of us, a worldview created out of our painful childhoods often pervades our adult understandings. We are in fact a collection of believed perceptions, anchored in a world of flesh based critical thinking. This is to say, we base much of our perceptions through the ever present flesh that Paul speaks of in Romans 7. Much more later, but for now the Bible tells us that the Word of God came to set us free. Free from what? Free from the negative implications of a performance based culture. Jesus is grace. He is all about grace. It is my observation, as a therapist for over 25 plus years that many Christians do not live in freedom; but rather live in a very unprocessed, complicated world, a world of unchallenged emotional "danglings".

These unprocessed thoughts, ideas, or patterns of life are partly created by our own fears of the unknown and unfamiliar territory of grace. When grace, often felt to be undeserved, is truly fathomed and comprehended as the depths of God's intentions, peace and absolute marvel are the byproduct of a relationship with Abba! We do not still ourselves enough, nor do we stop to ponder or gaze at ourselves; we move, go, and dart around almost unaware of knowing and being true to ourselves. We are people pleasers, true to act for others, but not to the pleasing of the Creator or the spirit that teaches us who we really are! We don't do this consciously, not at all. It is the subtle deception of the deceiver. So it is so critical that we read with intention what life really is all about… serving God to His glory. Peace is a formula, in some degree, of knowing whose we are, for whom we do "it", and how it is our "calling" models His mission for us! Fear stops our journey and we settle for the lesser journey, the path that is known and familiar.

I will speak more of "danglings" in the chapter on stress, but for now, the concept is a thought or injury that is historical or immediate, that is not processed, and is allowed to fester and create all kinds of wrong assumptions and mental images. It is a capsule of thoughts, a pocket of believed and practiced thoughts, destructive, and not true; or at least not true to the sense of who we really are! It is my hope that in the reading of this text, we can together create a new awareness of what it means to "live up" in an otherwise "down world". It is after all, the very Gospel message, that Christ died, paid the price, gave us the fatherly gift of grace, and has enabled us to become free indeed. Remember where it is we are going with these introductory thoughts. We are attacking the faulty thinking's of placing validation in anything outside the truth from God and that peace is to be "expected and anticipated". The way that we think creates the way that we live!

> *Christ said it is finished and finished it is indeed, just not in this our experience of daily grace.*

As we go forward in this process of living up, how do we "do" this or are we just to "become" peaceful by osmosis? Is it a five-step program? Is it as easy as one-two-three? I wish that growth and change was as easy as learning a formula, but it isn't. No, it is a process; a process often called sanctification. This sanctification is fully what God intends for us. In our reality, in our experience, sanctification is not complete, or at least to us it doesn't feel or isn't experienced as completed! This is somewhat of a "mysterious thought", but is genuinely true to the truth of God's sovereignty. Christ said it is finished and finished it is indeed, just not in this our experience of daily grace.

This is to say, that in Christ all things are finished, the process of growth is complete, but we, because of the flesh do not live in the reality of sanctified grace. We must be ever under the need of God, and in fact, this is a created design. God has given us over to a reprobate mind (Romans 11:32), this "good-for-nothing" mindset reveals itself in the areas of growth, or weakness (a term not used by this author), that we have residing in our personalities. What has already happened for us is that Christ has conquered for us every thought; however, our faulty perceptions, our sin, keeps us from fully believing and absolutely trusting God. At best, we can know the truth, apply the truth, and walk in the Spirit according to the truth, and yet still not realize the absolute freedom we already have. Such is the nature of a fallen, yet redeemed, world!

We have arrived in Christ! This truth sets us up for a peace or inner joy that can help us to stop striving and help us to rest in Him; or if you please, live up in a down world. What a blessing it is going to be to discover the joys that Paul spoke of in the book of Ephesians. Paul is saying in the first chapter of the book of Ephesians, that we are already in the heavenliness for which we were created, but that we have not yet become so on earth. We are already what we have not yet become. Wow! The excitement of the journey, though frightening and eye opening… begins now. Hallelujah! To God is the glory, for it is after all, all about HIM! A little more introduction of overarching principles and then toward the goal of personal peace and upward living we go!

Dr. Glenn W. Nowell, in his book, *Unconditional Joy*, says it this way: "Whenever I get upset or make a big deal of anything or anyone, other than God, I make a big deal of myself. You must relinquish your self-appointed position at the controls, this is not an option, and it is a requirement! When you relinquish control, you let go of guilt, anger, needless stress, fear, and anxiety. This is by no means an exhaustive list of the self-inflicted punishment from which you are released. You intentionally placed all the important things in life in the hands of the One who is able to handle them. All the positive results that you derive from the practice of these eternal principles are God's gift to you. It is a program of ego deflation in which God fills the void left by thorough housecleaning of the self-created clutter and debris that have kept you in denial, bondage, and separation from your Creator" (page 21).

> *As Aunt Maggie would always say, "A little bit better, yes, a little bit better everyday!"*

I believe that Dr. Glenn W. Nowell has captured it correctly. It is the essence and sense of where I want to go in this book. He based his thesis on the Beatitudes. Whereas, coming from the point of view of a counseling psychologist, who is also a pastor, I hope to create for the reader a believable, credible, and

Bible-based pattern for living life up in a down world. This pattern being proposed is drawn from key biblical concepts (paradigms), carefully interwoven with healthy psychological truths, producing an achievable inner peace.

"Be ye transformed by the renewing of your minds." All of this is a process of acknowledging the Word, emptying out the residue of our pasts, replacing them with the truths of the living word, applying them to our circumstances, and then seeking to examine daily where we are in the process, all the while being careful to ask those we trust for feedback and reflection. This is the premise of the book; the ability to live fully in what Christ has given us, peace and joy abundant! As Aunt Maggie would always say, "A little bit better, yes, a little bit better everyday!"

Overview:
Critical Concepts on the development of the "How-to's"

Before we go into the development of the content of "Living Up", let me share just a few more critical concepts behind what helped me to develop my thinking. In my understanding, for new thoughts to take root, they need to find healthy soil. This soil for me is composed of several indispensable ingredients: the conscious intended application of what we are learning, the want to change, the discovery of the motivation for change, and all of this, being fertilized by the scriptures of God alone! Let's look at these in brief overview before we proceed!

A. Consciously intentional discernment

Where are we going? Let's begin with this saying: Attitude, perspective, and the disposition you afford to life will determine, to a great measure, the quality of your life and the quantity of available time you have usable by the Holy Spirit. The ability to live in, yet above the circumstances of life, is determined largely by the way you think, your ability to stay "consciously intentional" with God, your understanding of yourself and the enemy's tactics to destroy your specific worldview, your ability to access personal peace, and your desire to give up personal control.

This is a statement that states we can not grow in Christ without a steady, aware, intended focus on Him! We can not really afford to be too casual with the study of the Word or the pursuit of His blessing for excellence. I believe, with very little energy, that I could take this statement and literally develop an entire chapter on this thought alone.

What is "conscious intentionality"? It is a coined term derived by me to say that life is lived by being aware and focused on purpose. In life, we mean well, but we must remember that living up in a down world and being able to live in, through, and not under the circumstances of life requires that we must be conscious about it, moment by moment by moment. We must learn to be on guard and alert to the activities of the spiritual world, and be careful not to underestimate the powers of the adversary. I would also be careful to say that the devil does not get the blame for everything; he is after all not all-powerful or all-knowing. It is not uncommon for the devil to be given credit for what just might be our own, often too casual, negligence toward obedience. This is to say become aware of the need for spiritual warfare.

A great exposition of this is found in C. S. Lewis' book, *Screwtape Letters*. We need to literally post in our cars, and in our living spaces, 3 x 5 cards that tell us the truth; little words or phrases that keep our minds stayed on what is true! I believe, with all of my heart that the adversary (Satan, the Devil, Evil) has but one goal for the Christian. He wants to take your joy, your peace, your patience, your kindness, your goodness and all those fruits of the Spirit and destroy them and make you believe them irrelevant in your personal walk. He wants us to be so lulled into complacency and that we do not even realize how undefended we are spiritually! How quickly our ability to live up is destroyed when we don't stay consciously intentional. I will offer much more on this concept later.

It is critical to my thinking that we stay awake, self-aware, and conscious of our thoughts, emotions, and derived assumptions. The consequence of failure in this "intentionality" creates bondage and a defeated sense, a feeling of deep inadequacy. This created inadequacy is the joy of all that is evil. The demons dance at the defeated downtrodden thinking Christian! This is why it is essential that we ask the Holy Spirit to help us with the difficult task of discernment. So much information presses in on our understandings, that without the mind of Christ, it is very easy for the Adversary to give us the wrong perspective and then create within us his desired negativism. I have tried to express the thoughts contained in this Greek proverb:

He who knows not and knows not that he knows not, is a fool; shun him!

He who knows not and knows that he knows not, is a child; teach him!

He who knows and knows not that he knows, is asleep; wake him!

He who knows and knows that he knows is wise, follow Him!

I think that this proverb is so very true! There is a great deal we could learn from this if we give it our attention.

In this saying is found an example of what I want you to understand about how and where we collect our perspectives on life. Some might say that this truth is not found directly in the Word. All that we follow does not have to necessarily come straight from the written Word. We can use our gift of discernment to glean from the world truths they derived from the truths of God's Word. This is a process that will help us to find a broader application of life, necessary for this very information complex world we live in. I fear too narrow a conception; if you disagree, that is fine, just remember that in a broader worldview we often gain context for the absolutes of the Word. Just a thought!

B. Scriptures for a basis/Soli scripturo

The "how-to's" of living up are all found demonstrated in scripture. I repeat this critical construct to give certain absolute understanding and power to the words of God. The Bible must be our source. The premise of the text is that all concepts are found demonstrated in scripture. They are not loosely, unfounded principles or theories; but rather, anchored in Bible based, actual phrases of the writers of the Book! It is important that we stress some key scriptures that have informed my thinking. What are some of these scriptures and how do they fit in the overall thought of the promised, intended will for us to have a positive life in this down styled and fashioned world.

To live is to enjoy God and to enjoy His creation. Look with me at some key scriptures that I've collected over the years. Each one of these was carefully picked as a scripture reference that serves as introductions for the basis of the entire text. As I stated earlier, critical to me is the concept of personal peace. I will cover this in Chapter 2. This personal peace is possible when we understand John 14. It states that God has come to give us peace, not a peace that we can create or manufacture, but a peace only he can give.

Subsequently, when we think on the things of Christ, bringing his thoughts into our heart (Proverbs 23:7 again), we then have the resources necessary to take captive every thought and make it obedient to Christ, the Peace maker. When we let go and let God captivate our minds (not TV or whatever), the result is a deep perceived peace, that only the Spirit can and does give. In Corinthians Chapter 10, versus 3 through 5, we find these words. "For though we live in the world, we do not wage war as the world does. The weapons we fight with are not the weapons of the world. On the contrary, they have divine power to demolish strongholds. We demolish arguments in every pretension that sets itself up against the knowledge of God, and we take captive every thought to make it obedient to Christ." (NIV)

Again, I'm not going to expound on this at this time. The details find themselves in chapters to come; however, these truths make sense to me. They are to me so self-evident, and I hope they will be clear to you as well. My point being, do we have them memorized? Are they part of our matrix of life? Do we believe them to be true? Do we call them so much the truth, that we have them as Psalm 119:11 would say, "Thy word have I hid in my heart that I might not sin against Thee." (KJV) Have we so ingrained this truth that when trouble comes, or when pain comes, or tribulation or stress occurs, we instantly have something to combat this feeling? This memorized scripture is then available to be recalled and used as a response to replace the reaction of the flesh. We learn to face fears by replacing the fear with God's Word, discovering where in our history it came from, erasing the thought by biblical application, and realizing that in fact, this process has caused us to erase and replace the fearful thought with God's Word. After all, the word of God sets us free, but only the word of God we know and apply can actually set us free!

Remember, however, that our freedom was accomplished on the cross, a finished work, not yet known in our flesh but available to us to help with our fear. If God has preceded us in His providence, there is no real need for worry. He has actually gone before us to prepare the path. He tells us He is in our lifeboat and we are going to the other side… period! What a peaceful thought. *We know this in the faithful application of scripture and the right thinking of shame free grace*! Later on I will speak about the concept of shame free grace and the weapons of spiritual warfare.

A curious side note: I don't always call it spiritual warfare, because many people are often frightened by this concept. People wonder if I'm seeing demons behind every bush. So, in order to ensure the concept is received without that judgment of fear, I have learned to call it scriptural warfare. That's the ability to combat non-truth with truth so that we can live up in a down world. An A creates a C, through our believed B's. Just a thought!

Another scripture that has been important to me in the formation of these "how-to's" is the scripture Philippians 4:8, "Finally, brothers, whatever is true, whatever is noble, whatever is right, whatever is pure, whatever is lovely, whatever

> *After all, the Word of God sets us free, but only the Word of God we know and apply can actually set us free!*

is admirable-- if anything is excellent or praiseworthy-- think about such things." (NIV) It's important to me that when we are living up in a down world that we keep our minds stayed on the things of truth. I'm not a person who wishes to be seen as holier than thou, but I do watch my path and influences carefully.

For example, I keep the radio on Christian broadcasting. I keep my television around things that are of good report. I don't want those things having time and space in my energy and I don't want them forming my opinions or perceptions of the world. I think you understand what I'm saying here. I strive to keep the positive, upward focus in my awareness. I am not saying that in the use of other influences comes necessarily bondage, but for me I prefer the discipline afforded by a concentrated vantage point. It provides less confusion for me. This vantage point must be based in believed, revealed truth from God. Notice the concept in the few verses to follow.

Mark Chapter 4, verse 35 says, "That day, when evening came, he said to his disciples, let us go over to the other side." (NIV) Later, we are going to discuss worry, anxiety, fear, and anger and how all these feelings tie in to living up in a world. To these issues or feelings God has given one of the finest answers. What he was saying here is, "Fellows, get in the boat, let's go over to the other side." This was a God "say-so", not an option that we *might* make it, but a "say-so of Christ" that we *will* make it.

In the middle of the journey, you may remember

> *This was a God "say-so", not an option of we* **might** *make it, but a "say-so of Christ" that we* **will** *make it.*

that the boat began to tip and bounce. While the Savior was still asleep, they woke him and said, "Are you not worried about us?" He instantly turned and rebuked them saying, "Why did you wake me up? Have you forgotten everything I've taught you?" They had forgotten that the truth of what he said to them was, "We are going to the other side, and you don't need to worry. I told you we were going to the other side." Thanks to my friend Dr. Dennis Sommers for helping me to discover this truth.

What they believed he said was, or at least their histories and believed perceptions created this thinking for them, that even though he said they were going over to the other side, surely he didn't mean He would even be with them in the storm; storms and wind kill! They drew their assumptions based on fear, which we all understand to mean, false evidence appearing real. What he said, in fact was, "We're going to the other side. You and I boys are going to the other side…period!" This is a perpetual thought guaranteed to produced peace! God will and is with us each and every trial and tribulation. He is the very air we breathe and He cares! When we can come to know and to internalize this truth that God is with us in this boat of life, it helps us base our life in what is actually the truth.

I don't know about you, but many times in my life I've lost sight of the other side. I have lost sight of the journey; I've lost sight of the passage for fear of the tribulations incurred while on the journey. I lost sight of the shore. I compromised my convictions and followed after my desires or wishes. I allowed fear, and my desire to be in control, to lead my mind in the direction of what I saw, rather than what God said. Often the desire to "not see" God's designed path is not so much in my error of thinking, but rather in my want to believe what is convenient to my desires. This is a popular philosophy of today called "relativism", where all is seen through what we believe rather than what God's Word says.

When we lose sight, we need to recall some scripture that is true for us. I don't mean this to be empty or for it to be a Christian syllogism that covers up tragedy and tribulation. I don't intend for it to be a Band-Aid approach, or a simplistic answer to a difficult problem; but rather we can claim a scriptural truth, apply it in the midst of the tribulation, and from the Word or logos of Christ, use our faith not to fix but to strengthen us in the ability to overcome and respond. It seems to me that our faith is not designed to keep us from things happening, but rather that when things happen, we can have the energy and the where with all to make a Christian response. Our ability to make a Christian response to the circumstances of life determines whether or not we live filled with joy and peace or whether we live life under the circumstances. *It is said that circumstances do not a person make; but rather, it reveals who they truly believe themselves to be.* In chapters to follow, I'll expound on the concept of personal peace, given to us by the grace of the finished work of Christ.

In the chapters to follow, there will be many more verses used to demonstrate that truth and psychology do not have to be counter to each other. This book does not intend to practice "psycho-babble", but will attempt to apply scripture to life issues. We will be talking about personal peace, how our perspective and attitudes impact our peace, some issues that we have to overcome, concepts for living up in a down world, perspectives and attitudes that defeat us, self-concept development, how to practice good stress management, learning to take each day as it comes, concepts for being content, developing a sense of altruism and optimism, using and developing a great sense of humor, understanding keys to life, and some final thoughts on how to overcome depression, fear, worry, and a poor relationships. A lot, yes but I believe it to be in brief and readable terms. Go ahead…I promise! This last thought before we journey together!

Elston Britt, a songwriter from the 40s wrote these words, " I'm living on the mountain in the good old gospel way, I'm drinking from the fountain where the living waters play; I'm feasting at the table with the master everyday, I'm living on the mountain--drinking from the fountain-- in the good old gospel way." I want to thank Rev. Buck Holcomb for having that record in his collection and for allowing a young boy to fool with his collection of records. It was that act of permission that has blessed my life for decades and decades. Thanks Buck and Betty!

Are we ready to live in the good old gospel way? Are we eager to be free of the guilt that so easily binds us? Do we want to walk in freedom and know the peace that only God through Christ has given? I hope so. It is my prayer that you will enjoy the journey and that the journey will be filled with peace, a peace that is created by right thinking and right believing as found in God's Word. Every situation in life has a biblical answer and a biblical response. In *Living up in a Down World*, I intend to address the challenges of living a positive life, in this not so positive world. Are you ready? I think so, or at least, I promise you're going to greatly enjoy the journey before us.

You're going to have to be your own best friend, you're going to have to put down old thinking and be willing to replace them with new concepts. You're going to have to bend your will, which is tough for most of us because we are so self-made and self-absorbed! The question then becomes, are we willing to bend our wills to the Master? Are we willing to open our hearts and minds and allow the Holy Spirit to do his job; that of, renewing our minds? Can we face the pains of the past and replace them with the hopes of the future. Let's go together on a trip, a trip designed to bend our wills to God and live in the "bornness" of His spirit. A trip designated for each of us to walk, a journey to find the greater story hidden within each of us. A journey begins with one step, so let's get on with the trip! Hold on Dr. Bob, what is the benefit or our reading on? What gifts await our further reading? Is the journey worth it? "Yah sure ya betcha! It's a keeper!" (Norwegian for yes)

The first benefit is that you will understand the importance and the role that Peace plays in the life of the believer. The ability to walk through life with the gift of Peace is exactly what God promised us in the Word (John 14:26-27). Yet, for so many of us, we walk life fearful, worried, over stressed, alone, and empty. The application of the thoughts here presented has given me the Peace that God promised.

Secondly, you will come away with techniques to use to literally wash the brain of the negatives that a fallen creation has placed there. You will look at the concepts for Living Up, each of which has been used to help me gain much of the identity and purpose God wants for my life. I don't necessary believe there is only one "something" God wants me to do, but the ideas shared have given me a peace about waking each day to the joy of the journey and purpose for the "sailing".

Thirdly, the applications of these concepts apply to all areas of need in your life. I will share my personal journey with anxiety and depression and demonstrate how the concepts have given me the victory over a dysthymic depressive disorder.

The certain application of biblical concepts and the auspicious use of psychology has set me free, and free indeed I am! This text is not designed to be a technical journey, but rather a personal experience of what has worked in my life.

Lastly, and certainly not the critical, pivotal point of the text, but… **the read will be fun!** When you have read the thoughts given here, it is my belief that you will feel better and have enjoyed the light journey of looking at life through a "much more lighthearted" window. A window of humor and dialogue designed to give you a "pick me UP" in the middle of life and all its struggles! I will attempt to share pictures, stories, anecdotes, and humor to help traverse the expanse of the seas before us…corny, sure, but you will "sea" what I mean in a little bit!

Section One: A Must Read

Chapter One:
A Prelude to Perspective / Living Grace"fully"

Is your glass half empty or half full? Are you an Eyeore, a Tigger or a Pooh? Do you wake up in the morning and say "Good Morning Lord" or "Good Lord Morning?" What thoughts could be said to pervade your mindset in the morning? Are we looking for the negative or do we position ourselves in the pasture, postured for the grace of God and His sufficiency. We are going to embark on the journey of learning the importance of perspective and attitude. For now, let me make my point in a general sense, and then later I will try to give specifics to the application and how's of a proper biblical attitude and perspective. It will also be important to look at some of the pitfalls that occur along the way.

> *The self same wind that blows one ship to Heaven, blows another to hell; it is not the force of the gale that determines the course, but rather the set of the sail.*

I will never forget the story of a poor young pastor working in the backwoods of Louisiana. It was a Sunday afternoon and his wife had become bored and she wanted to go shopping. As she started to leave the young man reminded her that their salary was very low and that he hoped and prayed that she would not fall victim to the temptations to buy anything that may not be real necessary. He shared his concerns with her and she stated it was not going to be a problem. Just in case she did become tempted, he reminded her of a lesson that they taught the children in vacation Bible school. When she was tempted she should turn around and say "Get Thee behind me Satan". This would then cause the temptation to go away and she could then go on with her pleasant shopping without spending.

So the afternoon went on and he fell asleep. Sometime later she arrived and she had in her hands one of those purple colored beautifully textured boxes. You could hear the sound of the tissue paper inside which told him it would probably not be a box from Wally Mart. Keeping his cool in not being upset, he asked his wife if when she was tempted, did see say, "Get thee behind me Satan". She looked at her husband and sheepishly said, "I did but he said it looked good from there too!" It really does seem to depend on your perspective, does it not?

The following statement is a pivotal saying in my experience. I will repeat it often and desire that you might memorize it for your own! "The self same wind that blows one ship to heaven, blows another to Hell; you see, it's not the force of the gale that determines the course, but rather the set of the sail." I first learned this saying from Colonel Sessions, a chaplain from the Minot Air Force Base. It has become a mantra for my life. I say it often. In fact, it sets up the very perspective and basis for the understandings of this book. The wind blows, but the set of the sail, which we determined, sets the course.

Parenthetically, I would say that this is not exactly true in North Dakota. If you ride a motorcycle in North Dakota, you're likely to end up in the ditch. I have, and I have come to appreciate the winds of the plains. I had nothing to do with pointing the wheel in that direction, or so I thought. Nonetheless, I ended up in the ditch! I sold my motorcycle for a dining room table, a gracious gift of a friend named Mike.

Oswald Chambers, states, "God has not promised us an overcoming life, but He has promised us a life of overcoming." The Scripture tells us in John 15:33 that in this life you will have trouble but take heart I have overcome the world. There is so much truth in this daily devotional thought by Oswald

> *We do not have to measure up, we already have!*

Chambers. I'll expound heavily on this topic when we come to the chapter on personal peace.

It is true that we are able to live beyond the circumstances and that we can live in the bigger faith journey. Paul teaches us that we are in fact more than over comers. The emphasis here is that in the act of overcoming, the more important concept is not that we are doing what it takes to be overcoming but that we are in our very being over comers. The not so subtle difference for me is in the fact of our "being in Christ over comers" and not focusing so carefully on doing the acts of what an "Over comer" does. The critical emphasis being on what Christ has and is doing in you through the Holy Spirit over against what we try so hard to do in our flesh.

We are so often fatigued and confused by the thoughts and imaginations of our own abilities that we forget that we do not have to measure up, we already have! In realizing His love, we want to measure up. We want to please the giver of the grace that gave us life and freedom. We respond to God

5

not from fear or reward, but rather out of a desire to please Papa, Abba, the Father.

What a peaceful place to live, the life of being empowered by the finished work of the cross. Letting go and letting the natural outflow of the Spirit reign in our lives. No pressure, just manifesting Him. It is being, not doing. Being is a reflection of what God has created. It is a reflection of the control of the Spirit. It is the response to life developed from "letting go". Doing is the emphasis we place in the need to please God. Doing comes from our histories of wanting to please and gain acceptance in our actions. We are accepted. Christ is our acceptance before God. Our doings reflect our want to thank and worship God for his free gift of grace.

When you ask me how I am doing, I'll often say I am "being fine". Peace is not in the struggling, Christ already has. It is not in the doing of good works, He ordained those for our pleasing Him (Ephesians 2:8-10). It is in the "being" of who He has already made us to be; thus I be's fine! Again, there will be much more on this later as this mindset is critical to the life God gave us, a life of peace and submission.

Let's demonstrate and state this in another way by referring to one of the great philosophers of the past. St. Francis of Assisi has said, "Having been shown the love of God, now love God and do as you please." What a delightful and intriguing statement he has made. One of the cornerstones of my life has been derived from this statement. I have realized that I cannot be motivated to service by guilt or by ought-ness. I must be motivated to service from love, in the realization that His gift of salvation is unearned and

> *Love does not need love, but desires adoration and appreciation of the "gift".*

unmerited and nothing I do gained it for me, and nothing I will do can loose it for me. I know this is controversial, but please read on. The thoughts of this text are valued, even if this statement is tough to comprehend...please read on! Motivation for our actions is the most important question we will ever ask ourselves. What motivates me to change?

If my motivation for serving God is not love, then it seems to me that it is necessarily found in having to perform in order to measure up. This sets up an ever-complicated process of trying to earn a father's love. God did not make us this way, we are not robotic. He wants us to respond to His awesome gifts in such a way that we can do nothing else but respond in love. This has been for me, one of the greatest revelations, a "revelization" or an Ahhah realized. I truly believe this is the most awesome, self realization I have ever discovered. He placed in me the ability to please and be acceptable to Him and for Him. Wow!

God wants me to awesomely worship him. Not worship out of a need or compulsion, but out of an breathtaking understanding of the gift God has given. Of all the things I've learned in the last couple of years, this is the most humbling--God thinks enough of me to give me his gift that I might have life. Not a gift that I have to earn or somehow pay for, but a gift given solely by His desire. It says in Hebrews chapter 10, verse 30, "Sorry will be the man who stands in the face of the living God." (NIV) Without the grace of Christ, I cannot imagine standing before God.

I want you imagine standing before God without the grace of Jesus Christ. It would be like standing in front of a 5000-degree fire! When I realized exactly

> *God thinks enough of us to give us His Son, that we may have life!*

7

what had been done, taking away my entire ego and all of my need to be in control, then I finally realized what Christ had and is doing for me. Life began for me in a new way and I came up with the title, *Living Up In a Down World*. We serve an awesome grace giving God, not a duty-bound works earning God. Satan uses all of his legions to lock us up in a "payback mentality" only to have us discover that there is never enough "works to payback". Satan, or life, or the pressure to perform, is never quenched! This concept is difficult for many of us because we have such a great need to pay something for what God has given.

In John, chapter 6, verse 29, the author tells us that in order to do the work of God we must simply believe in the one God has sent. Someone might ask, how can I work for God? How can I pay? How can I earn this gift? You can't! It's really clear in Romans 5:5 that you cannot pay back what God has done. So, what can I do? I can only respond. I can only review my life. I can only Reflect on what God has done, Respond to what he has given me, and I can Rejoice. The 3 R's of our proper relationship to grace! How do we do the work of God? By grace, we believe on the Son, the rest of it comes as a natural outflow, a response to his gift. I want to please my father because he has loved me and I love him. This is the perspective of grace, founded in freedom, a freedom not to strive; but rather, a freedom to relax in His striving through you. It is all about Him…Jesus! The perspective of grace is not a "how to" but an overarching, global perspective that covers all the steps later presented in the text. We set our perspective. At this point, I am not speaking about the perspective of how we look at life, but rather who gave us life. God's grace, properly understood, gives us the backdrop that makes it possible for us to do the steps of living up. Grace, faith in Christ, given to us by the actions of Christ, by the will of the Father is…Christ in us, through us, doing His will! Our response, necessary for living up, is in some ways responsive to our obedience.

In Hugh Prather's book, *Notes to Myself*, he says this: "I am convinced that this anxiety running through my life is the tension between what I should be and what I am. My anxiety does not come from thinking about the future, but from wanting to control it. It seems to begin whenever I smuggle an "I want to become" into my mind. It is the tension between my desire to control what I will be in the recognition that I can't, I will be what I will be. Where is the anxiety in that? Anxiety is the realization that I might not reach the rung on the opinion-ladder, which I have just set for myself. I fear death most when I am about to exceed what others expect of me; then death threatens to cut me off from myself, because myself is not yet." (Page 6)

I so agree with the depth of what he is saying here. Let me add this tiny afterthought. I will be best when I am what He feels is best. A father wants the best for his children and we kids fight so hard against what the Dad wants us to do. We want to be right, not Dad! Dads don't know everything you know! What a journey of struggle, a struggle against our strong self will and the desire to be in personal control. We so want self sufficiency and self reliance! I commend the book to your reading. Let's take this a little further.

Two stories emerge for me at this time. I've a friend named Pat. He loves his hunting dog. In fact, Pat could be said to believe in this dog. Pat shared with me that he enjoys watching his dog work. He enjoys watching the feet of his furry friend; literally patter with excitement, because he is doing what God created him to do. This joy did not come without a cost. Day after day after day, Pat took the dog and worked him in the field. When the puppy would loose concentration, he would wonder off, and if he wandered too far, the dangers of the road became a real problem. Pat would then gently correct the puppy, put him back on task, and watch the pup return to the joy of his pattering, excited feet.

What a joy it is to watch a creation of God, growing into the understanding of the joy of what God created it to be. Pat's dog does not have to earn the respect and love of his master, he does what he was created to do, and the master loves him. The real grace here is that even when the puppy doesn't perform perfectly, Pat loves on. Peace for the puppy is most complete when he has the heart to obey, when he sets as his life the learning of the message of his master. This illustration is not quite unconditional, but as close as this analogy will allow. The only true Master does love with an unconditional love…grace! This grace is grace without condemnation; a life empowered to live freely by the indwelling Christ's finished work on Calvary!

This thought might be helpful in making the point of perspective, grace, and faith I want to draw. When I draw the parallel between God and myself, I have come to understand God as my Father. I understand the need for inclusion here, and I know that the word Father does not in any way describe the awesomeness and vastness of the Creator, but for me, it is a workable semblance. The Father created me and he adopted me into his family. By the nature of this very creation, God wants me to be obedient and to follow his guidance. This is what a Father wants most from his son or daughter. When I do, life is good. Enjoy! When I'm disobedient, life is not so good. I still enjoy the privilege of the family, but my joy is greatly diminished.

Parallel this with my own children. I am their father, I chose them, and nothing they can do will cause them to be un-chosen. All I want is for them to understand the rules and do their best to follow them. My children's greatest joy will be found when they desire to please. What a father wants is not to have to enforce the obedience, but rather to hope it comes as a result of what and who He is. So, what we have here is the concept of life being lived in and through a proper perspective and a proper attitude. This is the entirety of the third chapter. Let me share a story to make a point.

About five years ago, enjoying an early snooze, I heard a high shrilled shrieking noise coming from my daughter's bedroom. She cried out, "I can't see my eyes!" I turned to my wife and asked her to be still because I believed all that Kristin wanted was my attention. I lay there quietly hoping for the best, but you know as well as I do, that a four-

> *What a father wants is not to have to enforce obedience, but rather to hope it comes as a result of what and who he is.*

year-old will not stop until they have met their need. In a matter of moments, she once again screamed, "I can't see my eyes!" At this point, I got up and immediately said to her, "I can't see mine either." She didn't think it was funny! Not even a little bit! I asked her what was wrong, and she once again told me she couldn't see her eyes. I asked her what she really needed because, after all, I mean really, no one can see their eyes, can they? Nay!

Promptly she shared she needed to go to the bathroom. I said, "Go ahead the bathroom is just across the hall". " I can't see my eyes!" With forcefulness in my voice, I told Kristin to go to the bathroom. She said she couldn't because she couldn't see the floor. Then it began to occur to me. She was afraid of what might be on the floor. I had forgotten to turn on her night-light. Everybody knows that on the floor of a four-year olds room are all kinds of monsters and goop and stuff. She indeed could not see her eyes and the fear of the floor was too much to overcome, bathroom or not! You see, had I not seen her perspective, I would have likely just turned around, left the room, scolded her and woken up to a wet bed. How incredibly important it was for me to see this situation through a proper perspective. This patience demonstrated in this situation is exactly the perspective we are going to need to make life work in a down world.

Of course there is a biblical point of view or perspective, and there is a world point of view or perspective. Let us take a brief look at some examples that illustrate the vast difference in the two perspectives. It is so easy for us to be caught in the rationalization of our views, for we so want what we want and sometimes at almost any cost. When we desire a particular sin, it is not difficult to "theologically rationalize". That then gives tacit permission to indulge. "Daddy, I want this! I need it to feel whole and OK!" This sets up the pattern of settling for the lesser than what God wants and we live a life of settled for lesser thoughts because of our own self created "worlds of indulging". There is so much being said here, but let this settle the point for now: When we respond to life in willful obedience, a peace that fulfills is the outcome! This you can take to the bank: proper perspective realized produces peace!

The world says we are just average and that most of us are not very happy, and that is what we settle for and call OK.

The adversary so wants us to be mediocre! The Bible teaches that we are made a little less than God, crowned with glory and honor. Psalm 8:5 (KJV) shares, "Yet thou hast made him (man) little less than God, and dost crown him with glory and honor".

> *The world says we are just average and that most of us are not very happy and that is what we settle for and call OK.*

Another simple thought to illustrate. The world's perspective is that it is not my fault. I'm not responsible. I am a result of a cosmic mistake and I cannot be held responsible. Some else is to blame. The Bible teaches that we are responsible. I am guilty but not shamed. It is the fault of choices I have made; yes often with inadequate knowledge, but choices mine nonetheless. This is shared in Matthew 12:36 and in Romans 14:12. The Bible does not stop with only the bad news of accountability, but also gives us the good news of redemption. The Bible teaches we are redeemed through the redemption of Christ. The world says I am a victim. The Bible teaches I am an agent of change. I am salt and light to the world. I am an over comer, made more than just a conqueror, but I am to overcome (Romans 8:39). The world's perspective is I must conform and expect very little out of life. The Word of God teaches just the opposite. Imagine that! The Bible teaches that we are transformed and can dare to dream, dream about the

> *Our perspective sets our worldview and thus our reactions to the conditions of life.*

wonders of God's plan for your life (Jeremiah 29:11). So, a proper, well thought out perspective is critical!

Before we go any further lets take a look at the goal, Peace! A peace that is so reflected in the scriptures of John 14. I wonder how full your peace-o-meter is. Much more will follow on perspective and attitude; especially the mechanics and the "how to's" of proper perspective discovery. I just wanted to "wet your whistle" about the absolute centrality of the concepts being framed in perspective. Our perspective sets our worldview and thus our reactions to the conditions of life thrown at us by the world and its leader, the Adversary, who walks around the creation seeking to kill and destroy the peace of the redeemed. The concepts laid out in the next chapter are the goal of Living Up!

Chapter Two:
Personal Peace-The End Result of Living Up

When I was a child, I had the joy of being with Dr. Billy Graham's assistant, Dr. Mooneyham. Dr. Graham was in Berlin to do a revival for the Protestant Men's group, a group where my Dad served as president. I remember thinking how special it was to be with someone my Dad thought so cool. I sat there listening to what he and Dad were talking about and what I remember is that Dr. Mooneyham shared that Dr. Graham believed that we could always look to our pasts with Christ and find the peace we need for the day. He called this looking at our "signposts". He shared Christ had given him a peace in knowing that once God had said it, and done it, it was true even when circumstances were more than we thought we could handle.

Signposts were for him little proven events where God had done as He promised and that you could count on the same outcome every time. I have grown to call this opportunity for faith, simply, "God's say-so's". The truth of this word is in Psalm 91 verse two. It says, "I will say of the Lord, he is my refuge, my strength, my fortress, and in him will I trust". (NIV) The key thought is that by saying what God says is true, applying it with faith, the result is a responsive peace to the challenge put before us. If I am afraid, I speak "no weapon shall be formed against me" and the resulting peaceful response is strengthened by saying and applying the Words of God. The precept here is the thought that what we speak and what we say are powerful reflections of the inner personal space. If we believe the "Say-so" of God, this then creates for us a reflective of His divine intentions and thus a positive "can do attitude".

I have said it before and I will say it again I am sure: this application must be conscious and intentional. We must always bring our thoughts back to God's truth and do it with a certain expressed thought. We must know the truth (and thus the need for Bible study), expressed in words to ourselves (or even better to prayer partners and study colleagues), confess it and bend our wills to apply this revealed truth to our lives (and thus discipleship). Scripture plus obedience plus time equals growth! S+O+T=G! This thought thanks to Dr. Hendricks!

A. Thoughts on Peace

These thoughts are essential to our understanding of personal peace. Believe in yourself and that God is in you to work his perfect will. We all have areas of strength and areas of growth. We only seem to remember our areas of growth (weakness). I have heard it said, "The great master fallacy of the human mind is that it compares itself to others; thinking more of others than it does of itself". Let us remember that God gives our gifts, and so it is He who will empower them -- let go and trust. Put life into

> *Believe in yourself and that God is in you to work His perfect will.*

perspective, faith and grace reign! God has and never will let go of the rudder. Don't ever give up, he doesn't on us, and we ought not on Him!

We can see life as an awesome unfolding of God's grace. Or we can see us struggling everyday for morsels of bread. The perspective is ours to choose, often that choice is not easy to make but the choice is ours. *Seek peace and be "other focused".* I believe that personal peace is the result of a life "lived up in a down world". We need to develop a strong sense of the spiritual in our lives. I'm not speaking of the spiritual as it might relate to a new age worldview, but rather to spirituality based in a strong personal relationship with Jesus Christ.

The word personal here is used to mean that the disciple believes, applies, and respects the truth that Jesus is both his Lord and his Savior. I am often asked exactly what is a "personal relationship". In two words, it is a "developed kinship". It is developed by time spend and it is a kinship resulting in one being brothers in Christ. Remember, religion is based in a relationship to a church or a denomination; but faith, is living in relationship with the person of Jesus Christ. We must see life as nothing more than living out our spirits to His glory.

> *Religion is based in a relationship to a church or a denomination; but faith is living in relationship with the person of Jesus Christ.*

David C. Needham says it this way in his book *Birthright*: "Sin is more pointedly, the expression of man's struggle with the meaning of his existence while missing life from God. It is all the varieties of ways man deals with and expresses his alienation from his Creator as he encounters the inescapable issue of meaning. Sin is a transgression of the law of God.

And to reject life, to determine a will differ from the will of God is the most heinous crime a person can commit. The essence of sin, then, cannot be separated from the issue of meaning."(Page 25) We are only significant as God chooses to give us some brief worldly significance. Remember this and peace will be yours!

Yet a few more keys are: *attempt to see the other's point of view and ask yourself what you can do to make the situation better.* This concept is the cornerstone of the therapy style of Solutions Focused work, remembering that the only point of actual influence to change is the ability to change ourselves and our actions. I would remind us to seek to encourage, intend to be extending, and seek to understand more than to be understood. Ask God to help you live life consciously and intentionally.

We need to live life with high intensity, "high passion", and go for the best of the gifts in our lives; yet, always live life with complete integrity. We must be true to God and then true to ourselves. What is on the inside must match what we do and say on the outside. This concept was made very popular by a therapist named Virginia Satire, in her book *People Making.* The concept of internal integrity is essential to finding personal peace. When we are not internally sealed with and seated in integrity, we diminish our self-concept, which sets us up to fail in any effort attempted at finding a personal peace.

We need to ask God to help us know where he is and what he's doing in our lives. We need to work on being more self-aware and on being more able to listen to the insights of our spirits. This is done by asking, and "wondering" at, the certainty of God's providence and his care. Providence says that nothing that happens to us is outside the influence and awareness of

God! After all, for me, this sovereignty of God is crucial and central to my theology.

Learn to respond and not react. Let our lives reflect that deep inner peace and not an artificial Sunday morning superficial reality. Love God and do as you please, which for the disciple is what he pleases. That is the truth and the truth sets us free and when we are free in Christ, we are free in deed! Free at last, free at last, yes, we are free at last! In the words of St. Francis of Assisi, "Now go and tell others about the love of Christ in your life, and if absolutely necessary, even use words".

Just a few more of the keys, and then we'll move on to explaining each and expounding on these ideas. In the explanations to come, there will be many more points made. These thoughts are serving only to give us an overview so that we can understand the framework in which I want to present personal peace.

Peace is found in the ability to stay connected to the source of our peace, God, and to His creation. Sociologists tell us that we need upwards of six support systems to be healthy. This surely must apply to spiritual health as well. For us to have peace, that deep and abiding presence of the certainty of his oneness with us, we must be around the things of God. Let me reemphasize, "S plus O plus T equals G"; a statement made popular by Dr. Howard Hendricks. This means, Scripture, combined with Obedience and Time equals the opportunity for spiritual growth. We must make the worship and study of God apart of our lives, prioritized and daily. When we do, the very Holy Spirit of God promises us a peace and contentment that we cannot create, given to us as the gift of God.

Another key, tied closely to this one, is that peace comes when we want to have peace. A word of caution here might be that I am not denying the sovereignty of God, but rather introducing the idea that within the will of God certainly falls man's volitional choice as to his everyday ability to access peace. We must allow the spirit of God to enter in freely and welcome his presence. We do this by prayer, pointing our feet in the direction of Godly pursuits, and willing our lives to be allies in, and to, His care. As I stated before, we must literally bend our wills to service of the Lord. Joshua said in Joshua 24 verse 15, "As for me and my house, we will serve the Lord". (NIV) So, let us live thankfully in peace with an attitude of gratitude and altitude. Remember, God wants to complete us, not just be a complementation as we see the need. Peace comes from him, through him, as we apply ourselves to the disciplines of the Spirit. God doesn't and hasn't made junk. He has chosen us to be at peace, but that

> *God wants to complete us, not just be a complementation as we see the need. Peace comes from Him, through Him, as we apply ourselves to the disciplines of the Spirit.*

takes more than a casual "vitamin supplement" taken at our leisure. The idea that peace will blossom in the field of "notional faith" is just not true. Christ promised peace to his disciples, not casual seekers of religious formality. The faith that grows the fruits of the Spirit is a faith that reveals the spirit within. Enough for now!

B. Attempts to define peace

This has been an overview of some thoughts on peace. Let us now take a moment to define the word peace and to explain how it exactly affects our living up in a down world. I found this to be more difficult than it first seemed. The world has so culturally defined the word peace that an effort at biblical definition is needed and yet somewhat complex and allusive.

Peace is a word with several different meanings in the Old and New Testament. The Old Testament meaning of peace was completeness, soundness, and well being of the total person. This peace was considered God-given, obtained by following the law (Psalm 119:165). Peace sometimes had a physical meaning, suggesting security (Psalm 4:8), contentment (Isaiah 26: 3), prosperity (Psalm 122: 6-7) and the absence of war (1 Samuel 7:14). The traditional Jewish greeting, shalom, was a wish for peace.

In the New Testament, peace often refers to the inner tranquility and poise of the Christian whose trust is in God through Christ. This understanding was originally expressed in the Old Testament writings about the coming Messiah (Isaiah 9:6 -7). The peace that Jesus Christ spoke of was a combination of hope, trust, a quiet in the mind and soul, brought about by reconciliation with God. The host of angels proclaimed such peace at Christ's birth (Luke 2:14), and by Christ himself in his Sermon on the Mount (Matthew 5:9) and during his ministry. He also taught about this kind of peace at the Lord's Supper, shortly before his death. This peace reflected comes from the most influential text, at least in my opinion, John 14:26 and 27. The apostle Paul later wrote that such peace and spiritual blessedness was a direct result of faith in Christ (Romans 5:1).

This word peace has been greatly influenced by culture and "new age" explanations. During a study I did some years ago, I attempted to define peace from as many aspects as possible. I confess that the list is not all-inclusive, but will give us some basis for understanding this difficult term so needed by the world today. In fact, this word peace is so needed, that humanity has seen a recent upsurge of spirituality. All finding itself in an unfortunate "new age eclecticism." My friend Dan Wolpert has much to say about this in his book, *Creating a Life with God*. The church, that which is referred to in Hebrews chapter 10, will find itself embedded in a miserable failure unless we offer authenticity and relationship within the walls of our buildings. For peace to be achieved, the two greatest needs of mankind must be met, significance found within security.

Peace is being at rest, emotionally and spiritually, with all above, around, and within. Peace is when all the water outside the boat is of little account. The trouble is when "our leaks" are admitted to the hold. Let not your heart be troubled -- trust -- I will be here. And I will be doing battle from the heavens on your behalf. Peace knows that Christ is working for you on the other side. Peace is the legacy of Christ; he doesn't counsel peace, he is and gives peace. Peace is a serenity of mind, where God rules your heart, and there you find a lack of trouble and fearfulness. Peace is a condition of inner tranquility that exists when we trust God wholeheartedly. It is when we accept unquestioningly His ordering of your life and lay your whole being at his absolute disposal. It is when we hold back nothing, make no reservations, and the result will be that we have a calm, steady, unafraid quietness of spirit. Lastly, but in no way finally, I offer some classical definitions of peace: 1) absence of war and strife, harmonious relationships, the goal of a Christian person's behavior, a proper orderliness; 2) describing a restoration of right relationship between God and man, peace through Christ, no longer alienated, Jesus is "Our Peace"; and 3) peace of mind or serenity, a lack of troubled and fearful heart, this piece is to rule our hearts. It is a framework of looking at life from a proper mindset and perspective. Being aware of the above saying might help!

I feel it is important to also state what peace is not, at least in the understanding of this writer. Once again, it occurs to me that perspective is incredibly important. I'm reminded of a story about a little boy, who said to a deacon that he loves the Lord. The deacon was a bit cruel and felt the need to play a little with the boy. The deacon said to the little boy, "I'll give you a dime if you'll tell me where Jesus is?" The little boy, not being discouraged, said in a very lighthearted way, "Sir, I'll give you a dollar if you'll tell me where Jesus isn't". Just a little humor to describe that in no way could I possibly describe what peace really isn't, but it might serve our purpose to try. How often have we been on the Pursuit of Happiness only to discover the Path of Destruction?

Whoa! Peace is not the object men commonly pursue -- pleasure, fame, and wealth are more like it. This pursuit leaves care, anxiety, and remorse. These do not meet the desires of the mortal mind, and they are incapable of affording that peace which the soul needs. I wonder if you could imagine for a moment the entire human race as though it were an art gallery full of picture frames. Long, long halls, billions of picture frames -- without any pictures! Empty. Some of the frames are very carefully carved. Some with delicate gold leaf and ornately decorated. Some rather haughtily painted. Others are dirty, chipped and broken. But every frame wrapped around -- nothing -- emptiness.

It is possible that God sees the human race in such a way, an art gallery with no pictures, just frames! Each human being was intended to frame an attainable, individual masterpiece of God's own reflected glory. But, due to mans' own want to self create, there is only emptiness -- a bare wall behind an ornate, man-made frame. To us the frames are obvious; however, the fact of emptiness is simply too devastating. It is not seen unless man practices "conscious intentionality" and acknowledges his fate. This is exactly what the enemy intends for man's thinking. And so humankind becomes obsessed with the only thing left to it -- its own flesh and self created bondage. How much we pursue the self-fabricated peace of our incomes, occupations, and bank accounts?

Peace is not as men of the world give. They salute you with empty and flattering words, but their professed friendship is often reined and has no sincerity. You cannot be sure that they are sincere, but I am says the Lord. The only absolute validation and genuinely sincere account of your worth and significance comes from understanding and internalizing the statements of God about you. The peace that comes from successes and building of treasures on earth is futile. The most significant aspect of this certain failure is that the sense of success is based in a world of uncertainty. There is no absolute; there is only relativity which bases the barometer for achievement of peace on external, non-eternal sources – other men!

For a thought or perception to be "absolute", it must by definition be based in an "absolute" source, and this is what we profess as Christians. The Word of God is the absolute truth and measure for our lives, and how we are to see life and live it! Peace is not a system or philosophy. This is often offered by false religions. False religions profess to give peace, but are not real. It is temporary and often seems more like happiness, which comes and goes with changing circumstances. It does not still the voice of conscience, it does not take away sin, and it does not reconcile the soul to God. Christianity is the only faith that goes directly to the issue of sin; thus finding peace in a relationship to the Savior.

Peace is about a relationship, not a religion. Peace is in fact; an element of our understanding that meets all the wants of the soul, silences the alarms of conscience, is fixed and sure of all external changes, and will abide in the hour of death and for ever. Again, let's not forget that the truth of God is not revealed to the intellect, but is delivered by the vehicle of the heart.

I was talking to a friend, Ken, about the truth and how we realize it. He made it clear that for him it was the revealed truth that God had given to his heart about life. It was not about books and philosophies because he said he was not much of a reader and his peace, which he has, came from within: a testimony of his heart and spirit. How desirable, in a world of anxiety and care, to possess this peace! Why would anyone not want this, especially when it cannot be taken from us... it is a gift of God.

Did you hear that, it can not be taken away from us? When the Adversary tries, we can practice "verbal aikido". This is a technique of deflecting the attack of mistruths and stepping out of the way of letting it be absorbed into our conscious reality. This is done by using some of the concepts of "spiritual deflection" later described in the text.

How is the term peace used in different senses in the Scriptures? Frequently it is a reference to outward conditions of tranquility, and thus of individuals, of communities, of churches, and of nations. It is a reference to Christian unity, implying the unions of one body, under one believe, and under one cross. It's deepest application, spiritual peace is a peace that restores the relationship of harmony with God.

Dr. Nowell says it this way, "The Hebrew word for peace is used so frequently inside and outside the Old Testament that its transliteration, shalom, is a familiar English synonym. In both the Hebrew, and its Greek counterpart, it may refer to something as simple as the absence of conflict; however, its basic and broadest meaning, when applied to a spiritual state of being, is wholeness. The natural craving for this wholeness is so powerful that every human malady can be traced to some sort of misdirection of its pursuit. Substances are used as an attempt to provide relief on demand. Hollow pursuits for meaning, excessive pleasure, and recreation spun out of control are those counterfeit and all too brief diversions discussed so frequently on these pages. Dysfunctional relationships provide anything but wholeness, and they fill the vast empty spaces only because they need so much room in which to malfunction."

He goes on to say, "Our role model is not an angel or a character from a parable or an illustration. Our role model is a real person in history. Jesus of Nazareth is the historical idea by which human wholeness is to be understood as the embodiment of 100% God and 100% human. Jesus Christ resides both in the intimacy of his relationship with his followers and beyond any subjection to intellectual examination. Nevertheless, the historical Jesus displays a variety of behavioral characteristics that together serve as a wholeness to be emulated. Jesus is our role model for peace." (Page 21)

Dr. Charles Stanley, in his book *Finding Peace*, makes these statements about trying to define peace. He states there are five essential believes that one needs to find a peaceful heart. Number one is recognizing and accepting the truth that God is sovereign over everything. God has never been out of control over his creation for one fraction of a second since the beginning of time. We may not completely understand God's purposes, but we can be assured of this -- God is still in control. In essence, God is absolutely sovereign, he is your protector, and he preserves your life from hour to hour, day to day, year to year.

Secondly, from cover to cover, the Bible has a clear message that God is the one who provides for all your needs. No problem is too massive, too problematic, or too severe for Jesus to meet it. The Bible tells us: "Those who seek the lord shall not lack any good thing" (Psalm 34:10, NIV). The need you have may not be a need for food, water, or clothing, but it may be a need for emotional healing, spiritual deliverance, a new opportunity for employment, reconciliation of a broken relationship, or any one of the hosts of other internal or relational needs. Peace is God's ability to meet that need. You cannot have peace and at the same time doubt that God will provide for you. Settle the issue once and for all in your heart and mind. God is your provider.

Thirdly, there are many things about your life in which you have no control. Accept those things as part of the way God made you and realize that God made you the way you are for a purpose. This has been strongly echoed by Rick Warren, as undoubtedly many of you know. You are a unique and very special creation of God, designed for a particular purpose on this earth that God has had in mind from eternity past. He tells us in Jeremiah that He has had our lives planned from the womb and He has good plans for us--good indeed! Accept who God made you to be! Learn to change what you can change, never stop growing in character, reject the lies you may have been told, those "danglings" of hurt placed by many in your childhoods, and accept the truth others speak to you.

Fourthly, a person who feels unwanted, rejected, or continually lonely is not a person who has peace deep within. Peace is a feeling that we belong to someone or to a group of people whose love for us is vital for our inner peace. Everybody on earth wants to be loved and to love someone. God tells us plainly that we are to have fellowship with other believers in the church. So it is that God has a place where you truly belong. Remember that the book of Hebrews admonishes us to not forsake the gathering of the peoples of God. Lastly, for real inner peace, to be defined and experienced, a person needs to know that he or she is competent, able, capable, and skilled at doing something. God did not and does not make junk! The "something" may be a task that the world as a whole considers to be a menial chore or service. Nonetheless, if you can do that task, and you know that you do it well, you're competent. God has a plan for your fulfillment. What an awesome five statements, all found in Dr. Charles Stanley's book, *Finding Peace*, a New York Times bestseller.

Possibly the most significant need this generation has is that of establishing and maintaining strong, secure, and meaningful relationships.

In trying to define peace, I feel it essential to add to the definition an attempt at framing peace within the context of faith. Faith is in and of itself a difficult arena for definition. A faith not found in balance can do more damage to personal peace than almost anything else I can imagine. The blockage that was most severe for me was the blockage of an "ought" faith as over against the balance of an "awesome" faith. As I earlier stated, an awesome faith is one that is appreciative of what Christ has done and works within that appreciation to please the Father, but not to try and measure up.

A faith that is founded and established in an ought relationship finds it must try to measure up, perform, and do enough to be saved. Never will, never can echoes the words of Christ when He said if we fall in the slightest, we fail it all. This striving created for me a faith journey that stopped well short of any form of peace. In fact, it was an impossible position that I could never fill, and so it was that I would rededicate and proclaim Christ as Lord over and over and over again. This in and of itself is a fine and required element of the journey. This idea of rededication is not bad, valuable in fact, unless it comes from a sense of worthlessness in our doing for God. We can not and will never be able to measure up enough to have peace. We then try to fix our pitiful selves by the approach of constant contrition founded in a low self worth and not founded in a strong rest in the grace and faith of God. We make errors and mistakes, but we are not a mistake needing to go forward again and again. What we need is the realization of the "who we really are" and to learn to live in that wholeness!

C. A friend's definition of faith!

The role of faith is essential. I alluded to this in the introduction. I believe the proper understanding of faith is so important that I want to use a paper given to me by a friend, Pat Holien, from Minot, North Dakota. The following is his definition, to which I heartily concur, of a faith necessary to produce peace.

"Faith, I believe, is not found in us, or by us, but is a gift of God. As it says in the first chapter of John, belief in Jesus is not of blood (inheritance), nor of the will of the flesh, nor of the will of man, but of the will of God. I believe we are not the creators of our faith, but rather God is. Jesus said that which is born of the flesh is flesh and that which is born of the Spirit is Spirit. The Spirit of God, the Holy Spirit, by the power of God is the creator of faith in us. In Romans 10 it says that faith comes from hearing and hearing from the word concerning Christ. I believe God imparts faith as he chooses and in the way he chooses. In the first chapter of John it says that in the beginning, the word was, and the Word was with God and the Word was God, and the Word became flesh and dwelt among us. Jesus is the word, Jesus is Go, by the power of himself, he can cause us to receive the word concerning him and receive the truth about him, creating faith in us.

Man from his very beginning stands against God. God created man to have a perfect relationship with him but he also understood that man would choose not to follow the way of God. Man chose not to follow God, and by the promise of God man became spiritually dead and was cast out of the presence of God never to return to him of man's free will, as man's free will to choose God was now dead. All of mankind was doomed to eternal separation from God because of sin or better stated unbelief. So, what is man to do? What is the purpose of life if it is to end and all that is beyond that is eternal separation from God?

God created us to have an eternal relationship with him and he has promised the means by which man can have that relationship. The means, the Way, the truth, and the life are all found in Jesus. The Word says that no one comes to the father except through the son and that the son of man must be lifted up that whoever believes may have eternal life. It always comes down *to faith. Man cannot and will not make himself right enough to ever be pleasing to God and receive eternal life with him. The only righteous flesh ever to dwell on this earth was Jesus, and it pleased God to offer his son as a sacrifice that by the shed blood of the perfect lamb, Jesus, man could be washed clean and made perfect in God's eyes. God did not send his son into the world to judge the world, but that the world should be saved through him. The truth is God has provided a way to be saved; he has provided us with his son, the Word, and faith. We can continue in the way of denial and unbelief or, we can receive the Word of truth and through the faith, which God has provided, believe and have eternal life with the Father.*

We may, by denying truth, believe that by our efforts we can somehow get it right and be acceptable to God, but if we are honest, we know this is impossible--it cannot be done. In fact, God says the flesh is so rotten that it must be destroyed and he will give us a new body and have been. He also says that there is no profit in the flesh, and that the best it can produce is but filthy rags before him. So, we can deny the truth that salvation is of faith and faith is of God and we can spend our entire lives on this earth trying to get it right and work ourselves into the grave trying only to find the best we could produce was nothing -- nothing of eternity. Or, we can receive the truth, Jesus, and know he is the only way, the only truth, the only light and life and we can have eternal life with the Father, Son and Holy Spirit.

Faith cannot come from intellect, study, or knowledge, for God says your ways are not my ways; my ways are higher than you can attain. Here it he says, if you think you are wise, I will confound your wisdom and bring you down with the lowly and I will lift the lowly to my dwelling place. So again, salvation is based on faith and faith alone, simple faith as of a child. As Jesus said, speaking of the children, that this is how we are to come to him. I do not know how I believe this all to be true, or how I came to believe all of God's work to be true, except that God caused me to have faith and by his doing, I received it. I thank him for it every time I think about it and I also question, study, wonder and debate how it can be true, but always by the grace of God come back to this, faith is of him, by him and for him so he may be glorified.

I am constantly trying to correct the weaknesses in my flesh, and for every time I think I succeed, I fail in ten more areas. But, because God tells me how I should live, I will continue to try, but not out of desperation and fear. God says that by the shed blood of Jesus all my sins have been removed from me as far as the east is from the west, so rather, out of love and obedience, and that not being of my flesh, but rather Jesus in me. In Hebrews 11:1, it says; 'now faith is the substance of things hoped for, the evidence of things not seen'. I think that says faith is not what we can prove or totally understand but rather just the opposite, that we are given the power of God in Jesus to trust in that which we cannot understand or prove but rather hoped for; the whole being provided in the word concerning Jesus, which gives faith. I write these words in love, and please understand that I mean it to give comfort and to bring you peace in knowing that salvation is not of our efforts but of God's grace through faith in Jesus." Pat

I think it wise to stop for a second and state why and what I strongly agree with in Pat's thoughts. I know it is critical to the concept of peace for these thoughts to be absorbed, processed, and made a part of the matrix through which we think our lives to exist. If not, we base our cornerstone on a shifting base of perceived perceptions which are so reflective of our current feelings, thoughts, and reactions to those thoughts. We would be only as stable as our current emotions and that is just not the basis of Peace. Peace is His gift created in His timelessness of promises and truths anchored in His Word given through His Spirit. Peace is the result of a believing, acted out faith walk with God! Too simple or direct, I think not! I agree strongly with these points. I would ask that if you disagree, take out the Word and let your mind mull over the thoughts, and ask the Spirit to give you a discernment that is broader than your exposed realities.

Growth is all about allowing and receiving new truths from the Spirit that challenge and possibly conflict with your current beliefs. This is the conflict between the spirit man which is yours by Christ and the spirit of the flesh which always wars to give credit to man. My relationship to God has undergone many subtle changes, each a challenge to what I just knew was true. So, give it a try! Salvation is a gift of God, caused to be heard by Him. It is His authorship to give and thus it can not be lost by us the gifted, only by the giver. A gift can be lost only if we have the power to loose it. We don't in this case. It is His eternal and unchangeable gift to us. This flies in the face of man's desire to control his destiny; but in this, gratefully, we have no domain of change. The gift of sonship and eternal rest in Heaven is not ours to earn, nor is it ours to loose! Human nature is to be in control. Human nature is a want to payback or earn rewards. As children, everything we had appeared to be earned; all except the unfathomable love of our parents, even in the face of us being us!

The choice that God has allowed in our experience of selecting God as our answer must always come through the atmosphere of God's sovereignty. Look at the Word as expressed in Romans 11:29-32: "For God's gifts and his call are irrevocable. Just as you were at one time disobedient to

God have now received mercy as a result of their disobedience, so they too have now become disobedient in order that they too may now receive mercy as a result of God's mercy to you. For God has bound all men over to disobedience so that he may have mercy on them all."

In the final analysis, all of us are absolutely dependent on God. He is the source of all things, including our destinies, our salvation, and our selves. He is the power that sustains and rules the world that we live in. And God works out all this through His understandings and to His glory. It is all to His glory and to the glory of His only begotten, Jesus. This is all-powerful and it is God, to whom is deserving of our praise. It is a hard truth, but if we base our existence on anything we designed or fashioned, it can only fail to sustain. By the way, notice the word irrevocable...curiously sustains eternal security, doesn't it! This is the ultimate and final will of God, that He has given us the gift, all or many is not the issue here; but that He has given it...period...irrevocable and unchallenged by the receiver...us!

Finally, it is not of the intellect. This faith is not a process of asking the questions and then providing the necessary answers by the application of good thinking or reasonable hypothesis. Karl Marx said it was nothing more than a created opiate for the masses, a designed contemplation to help sustain the weakness of insufficient human beings. Faith is a matter of trusting God in His effectual calling of His to himself. The word effectual is to convey that what God intends, happens. The unique greatness of His conception is that even the ability to believe and sustain is in His gift. In other words, faith is His Spirit giving a gift of His making and the very power to believe is His creation as well. We can wander off, but we cannot hide.

I went through a deep valley during a past depression, threw my Bible against the wall and declared God was dead to me. This lasted for over three years, during which time I did everything I could to disenable His call and power over my future. I stopped all activities of church, no reading, and no faith development. I declared war on this fanciful God image! Oh well, He is back!, and am I glad! Hallelujah! He states that He will never leave us or forsake us. Yea though we walk through the valley of the shadows of death, He is there.

Thanks for listening to these thoughts, it is critical to the concept of Living Up that we understand the author and finisher of our faith is God. When Christ said it was finished, He said it is finished. Nothing we can do affects the call of God on your life. The call is His, and yes, we can frustrate our lives by not being obedient; but the call of God is secure and anchored not by actions but by the promises of Christ. Please try to see this and ask the Spirit to reveal it to you. It is the Peace that we can not create and that only He can and does give.

D. The How's of Personal Peace

1. Symptoms of Inner Peace

Are we rivers of life, or are we too leaky? Do we not understand that we cannot heal ourselves? What is the operative force in our lives, our strong self-will's, or the spiritual work of Christ working through the Holy Spirit? How will we answer this question determines to a great deal whether or not we experience personal peace in our lives.

What are the symptoms of inner peace? In order to define peace maybe it would be valuable to take a look at some of the symptoms of peace. We can't know how until we know what it looks like. Much of this list is an adaptation of a list made by Jeff Rockwell in conjunction with his wife. I saw an amazing similarity to my list and I felt I could blend the two into one.

Inner peace could be defined as a tendency to think and act spontaneously rather than from fears based on past experiences. Often, we censor what we feel and say. In an effort to present what we hope is acceptable to others, we present a pseudo-personality or a false front. This mask we wear to please or appease others results in distress, manifesting the image of an outwardly, collected, got-it-together personality. Deep inside us, however, we know the difference. This difference comes across as being in genuine, and the effect it has on our self-concept is negative. When we are not true to ourselves and present only a likable personality, this causes incongruence. Others may not see it, but we do. The adversary uses the mind and takes this and developes it as another weapon to tell us that we're nothing but an old flat river worm, a nobody! This though process both confirms what we've been told by others and validates what we believe to be true about ourselves in the first place. This again is the "tiny bat" syndrome!

Peace is an unmistakable ability to enjoy each moment. It is the ability to live in the now. Christ tells us that he is taking care of the past through forgiveness, that he is taking care of the future with hope, and that

> *What is the operative force in our lives, our strong self-wills, or the spiritual work of Christ working through the Holy Spirit? How we answer this question determines to a great deal whether or not we experience personal peace in our lives.*

we are to live in the now by trusting. It is trusting with the simplicity of a child just as the birds of the air trust that God will feed them each and every day. So much of our peace is lost worrying about or fretting over what has happened and what might happen. Countless times I have ruined my day by not living in the moment.

My history has taught me that the joy of the journey is almost always lost in the fear of the trip. We live in the anxiety of the unknown future. It is a hard learned life lesson that teaches that growth in peace occurs as a result of the climb and not by living on the mountain, looking down at the valley in fear. The practice of being an unanxious presence is critical.

It has been said that when you're in the room; make sure you are really there. Or to put it more succinctly, when you are in the room stay there! God is not going to take away our weekdays because we fret and hope for Fridays. He might even shorten our weekends if we continue worrying about Monday morning! How many days we waste worrying or living in what we can't control or in what we can't change! The only thing we can change is ourselves, and how we feel and respond to the now.

This reminds me of a story about a little girl whose daddy had just come home from work. The daddy came home and immediately sat down in his easy chair and began to read the newspaper, taking a little time to relax and collect his thoughts; whereupon, the little girl ran to her mother and said, "Daddy's home". The mother looked at the little one and assured her that daddy was not home. "But Mommy look, he is sitting in his chair". With a clear and wise voice, the mother knowingly said, "No dear, he may seem to be here, but he's not!"

So often we find ourselves worrying about the future or obsessing over the past that we do not enjoy the moment that we are living in now; is this where you are? This inability to stay in the now costs us a great deal of personal peace. Start noticing when you're not living in the moment, acknowledge it, own it, and bring yourself consciously back to the joy of the presence of the current moment. For all we really have control over is the now (always acknowledging God's providential care). Now is it! Stop for a second and acknowledge the now and settle in for a time of meditation on the now! Stop, get still, think, observe, and proceed with the thoughts of the now ever-presence of a caring God. So much peace is maintained and generated by living in the now.

Other symptoms of peace are a loss of interest in judging others, intending to extend, and in "good finding." It is a loss of interest in conflict, giving up the need to win, and seeking to always ask what you can do to make the situation better rather than always blaming the other for what has occurred. Peace is a loss of interest in interpreting the actions of others. It's not taking other people's inventories, but rather focusing all in what you can do, being solution focused, rather than blame finding.

These symptoms seem to all fall into one category, a larger concept of doing what I call "being other focused". Who we are is not so important, as who and what we think others are. I read a quote one time that said this, "It's is not so much 'who we are' that counts, it is what we do with the 'who they are' that counts". This strategy of being other focused is critical to the overall personal peace of an individual. When we can focus on others, we become much less egocentric and we concentrate on lighting the candles of those around us and I believe we are blessed for having done so. "One candle, like a single word or phrase, may not light a dark room, but it can kindle the candle next to it, and the next and the next, until the room, like the heart, is bright."

Being other focused is a form of humility that serves peace well. This is not to say that we don't work on our own self-actualization, but as we are climbing the ladder of success, why not help others up as well. Life is not peaceful spent stepping on others toes as we climb to a self-made prominence. Remember, your success is only as sure as God's blessings. You are not what you have made, but are what He has given by grace. Don't get caught up in your successes, bless and focus on others as well. A truth easily said but one easily forgotten or misplaced in the moment of the ego!

Yet another symptom of peace is the loss of the ability to worry. This is a very seriously missing symptom. Inner peace is characterized by frequent, overwhelming episodes of appreciation. It is the walking around in your everyday lives and looking for the best in others, stating it to them in an appropriate way, and realizing that much of who we are is only discovered by the positive comments of other people. We, as individuals, have been blinded by the culture and the Adversary, to not allow ourselves to believe well of ourselves. After all, remember not to be haughty; pride cometh before the fall, and boy do we not want to fall. We have the power to bless but we so often withhold it, not out of malice, but because we are not staying consciously aware of the need to bless. We need to wake up each day in the blessing of the Lord, thank Him for the beauty of the day, and insure that we bless others in turn.

It's the ability to walk around being collaborative, seeking to please rather than to be pleased, and being your own best friend. It is the desire to understand more, and to be understood less. Peace is being connected with others and with nature. The greatest need of today's culture is the need for relationship and meaningful connection. We insulate ourselves with our "adult toys" and cry out we are so empty. The empty often comes from the isolation, all coming from fear and the development of the false religion of self. Essentially, we need to connect. People are not in need of things. They are in need of others. The working together is the essence of what community brings to the formation of peace. The 'I' works with the 'we' to form the 'us' that reflects the 'thee'. This is the very image of the Trinitarian sense of 'Us'.

Peace has the symptoms of frequent attacks of smiling through the eyes of the heart, having smiling eyes. I remember a video that impacted me greatly and in the video the presenter was making the strong point that when we are excited about what we are doing, it is a passion that overflows into the eyes and it appears that we are so joyful the eyes shine and glisten. This attribute or symptom of peace is found when we discover our gift and use it to the glory of the body life. We can only find deep peace when we are using our God given talents within the Kingdom.

I spot it the most when I look at the choir at our church. Under the leadership of Dr. Ken Bowles, the singers reflect his joy and show it in their eyes. They sing to the glory of God and they are using their gift to His glory. It is not a performance, but a realization of whose they are and for whom they were made to shine! Peace will be yours if you have an increasing susceptibility to the love being extended by others as well as the uncontrollable urge to extend it to yourselves. So, enjoy your shining eyes, and forget that you were always told not to be too happy; it will seem you are arrogant and "special". Aren't we…Special!

Peace, or least, a symptom of peace, is an increasing tendency to let things happen rather than to make them happen. It is letting go and letting God, giving up the need to control, and allowing the Holy Spirit to do in us that which we cannot in ourselves do. We so discount the working of the Holy Spirit. Many in today's culture are afraid of the Holy Spirit. Many feel we have over emphasized the work of this part of the Trinity, and so we throw out the baby with the bath water. Trust is the key here. Do we trust God to be who and what he said he was? I have come to understand God as the very air that I breathe. He is far more than a religious ideation or a foxhole illusion, or even a mother and daddy given Christ; but is rather the very essence and meaning of my life. In ways that are as biblical as possible, this deep sense of God as "Papa" has come with time, tribulation, and testing. How true I wish it was that God being my breathe could be at a lesser price.

Rockwell concludes his list of inner symptoms of peace, by implying a warning that if you have all or even most of the above symptoms, please be advised that your condition of peace maybe so far advanced as to not be treatable. What a joy and what a peace it is to find these characteristics in your life.

Here is the dilemma: earlier I addressed through the writings of a friend the importance of the biblical and proper understanding of faith. The following thought by Oswald Chambers will help to illustrate why that was important to the concept of personal peace. He says that sin is a fundamental relationship; it is not wrong doing, but wrong being. It is deliberate and determined independence from God. The Christian Faith bases everything on the extreme, self-confident nature of sin. Other faiths deal with sins; the

Bible alone deals with sin. The first thing Jesus dealt with was the heredity of sin. The sin heredity is an independent nature from God. In order for us to understand the how's of personal peace, it's important that we understand what Oswald Chambers was trying to say here. Christian faith is not based on following the law by trying to do right, but rather on understanding that we are right because of Christ.

The very subtle nature of this "apparently evident truth" is the very paradox of peace reception. All of us know grace is a free, unmerited gift. Nonetheless, our entire world, adult and childhood, was formed on acceptance based in merit and performance...good job thus good boy! God's economy says good boy who then does good job. The job is entirely the work of Christ in us. The struggle for peace is our deep, deep need to please! We already have, but we wonder, really God...grace?

So it is our faith is based not in doing but in being. The fundamental dilemma of personal peace is that we try, in so many ways, to create our own atmosphere of peace. Let me give an example. I've had the pleasure of being able to speak to numerous numbers of adolescents over the past 10 years, and at each of these presentations I've asked the question, "What is the key to happiness?" Almost uniformly, boys will tell me that it is the ability to make money; girls share that beauty reigns! So immediate and so self-reliant are these responses that it baffles me. Oswald Chambers is very correct here when he states that in order for us to have peace we must face the problem of independence... independence from God -- sin. We must understand that God wants for us relationship with His Son. Life abundantly is about returning to right relationship, focusing on Christ, and understanding the fullness of Grace!

Personal peace is possible when we make an unqualified commitment to the Lordship of Christ, followed by a desire to bend our wills to the leadership of the Holy Spirit, and then work to fill the commands of Jesus through choices coming from the fruits of the Spirit. We do this best in community, by practicing mutuality, collaborative action, and forbearance. We need to walk with each other, for peace starts with the walk. How very far our current culture has moved from this perspective!

To a large degree, we have given up the gathering of the Saints. Many have said we do not need the gathering, the cost of the building is foolish, and my needs are not met when I go. I can worship anywhere, in the woods, fishing, or just reading the Bible at home. Of course the problem with this approach is that in our own self-imposed exile, no fresh and new material is presented. We only circle around the same camp we've always believed. It is in the hearing of the word preached and in the community of the saints that we experience the colonization of new ideas. It is in this mutual sense, we learn from each other, we are challenged, and we grow.

We are also encouraged to make an unqualified commitment to Christ. By the very gathering of each other in support, we face our shame in a non-toxic way. Within a safe community of healing, we experience the joys of healthy remorse, repentance, which in turn leads to a deeper commitment to the Lordship of Christ. Through repentance, we recognize the joy of having forgiveness and then spend our energies on praising the

> *Personal peace is possible when we make an unqualified commitment to the Lordship of Christ*

God who gave us grace! This is a by-product of the support of the church in body life!

2. Personal peace begins with the proper perspective!

A critical question is, how do we choose to see life? Parallel to that is what is our motivation to live life well? Consider the case of two salesmen. One was assigned territory that had produced very little business for the company. This territory had the reputation that nobody can do anything with it. The man went to his new territory in full acceptance of the general appraisal that there was no business possibility there. So he reasoned," Why knock myself out? Having this no producing area hung around my neck is unfairly treating me."

You will not be surprised to know that he failed to develop any appreciable amount of new business and left the company. He never even gave it a try. It was for him, a fact that no opportunity was available there. His perspective toward it was negative. Result? Negative! A second salesman, brought in from across the country, knew nothing about the territory accepting that it was centered on a thriving metropolitan community. No one had told him that it contains no sales possibilities, so he proceeded to get busy and made many sales. "Why, this is an uncorked Goldmine!" All his thinking was positive and his activity was positive. He made a great success of the territory. But so profound was this man's positive mental attitude that had anyone told him it was a bad territory he wouldn't have believed it. And why should he?

Personal peace does indeed begin with the proper perspective. We ask ourselves how we choose to see life. Do we give in to our basic personality, or do we strive to become what God intended us to be, a new creation transformed by the renewing of our minds. Are we Eior, Tigger, or Pooh? Of course you recognize these as being characters in Winnie the Pooh, each of them having their own distinct personality. Eior is always saying, "I don't care, and it will fall off anyway." He is filled with despair and he looks at life through a half glass empty.

As a therapist, I could always determine the worldviews the person had by simply asking the question, "When you look outside the window, tell me what you see?" If the person said they saw a dirty filthy snow, I knew they were probably a pessimist. If they saw the beauty of the sky and the potential of a new snowfall, I knew I wasn't dealing with an Eior.

Tigger is your classic obsessive-compulsive overachiever. He goes around saying, "the most wonderful thing about Tigger's, it is that tiggers are wonderful things; they're bouncy, bouncy, fun, fun, fun! The tops are made of rubber and their bottoms are made of springs, but the most wonderful thing about Tigger's is that I'm the only one!"

Then of course there's Winnie the Pooh. He is so lovable and cuddly, and ever so needy! He is your classic people pleaser, always finding the need to make others happy so that he will be liked. He suffers greatly, or maybe just a little, by allowing others to tell him who he is. Anytime we allow others to validate our worth, we are placing our self-image in the hands of others and stripping ourselves of our own self-validation. Our validation finds its real foundation in the fact of our being chosen by Christ. We are His workmanship! This will always succeed. So we ask ourselves how we choose to see life.

How we choose to see tribulation or stress is another key for personal peace. Let me remind you of a quote I used earlier from Chaplin Sessions. "The selfsame wind that blows one ship to Heaven blows another to Hell; it's not the force of the gale that determines the course, but rather the set of the sail". In Galatians 5:22, we are encouraged to seek love, joy, peace, patience, kindness, goodness, faithfulness, gentleness and self-control. Here the emphasis is in looking for the affirmers in life, the positives, and the best way out of the storm. It is the seeing of problems as blessing. Blessings are after all the way that the spirit grows. Those who grow best expect stress, and they know that good things do not always happen to good people. They learn to expect "bumps in the road." These bumps, in turn create opportunities for growth. They create opportunities for insight. Insights create the ability to make empowered choices to change and change is what defines best the level of stress one undergoes.

As we are choosing how to see stress or tribulation, the following truth might find itself invaluable. Take a close look at this truth and see what it has for you. Maybe pause just for a second, reread the statement, and assess where you could apply some truths that you see in the statement.

We cannot control the stressors or events of non-peace that come into our lives, they just are. The feeling and thinking comes in freely. They may not be controlled initially, but we can control our thinking and our doing by carefully and consistently applying practices of faithful thinking and righteous doing. Non-peace exists when our worldview prevails over His worldview.

When we allow this to happen, the result is a worldview of relative truth supported in new age philosophy and eclecticism. This man created worldview fosters the pursuit of personally fabricated peace, a peace that never brings fruit. Scripture reminds us in Philippians 1:6 that we can be confident of this one thing, that He who began a good work in us will carry it on to completion until the day of Christ Jesus. Any self fabricated peace, sets up the great human dilemma, that of the war of the "Great I Am" versus the "Great I Can". The classic battle between God and the will of man is on!

I wonder, can we learn to see tribulation as an opportunity for gaining insight to ourselves? Can we see stress not as a catastrophe, but rather as an opportunity? Peace comes through the management of our tribulation under a deep understanding that God has overcome the world. Perfect peace is stayed on him who concentrates on Christ. Dr. Larry Crabbe states that many of us place top priority not on becoming Christ like in the middle of our problems but on finding happiness. I want to be happy, we say, but the paradoxical truth is that I will never be happy if I am concerned primarily about being happy.

So we must ask ourselves, "Why do we want to solve the problem?" When the problem is before us, how do we look to solve it? Peace is never resultant, answers are never found, unless and until we bend our thinking to model revealed scripture. The answer must be that we are only more like the Lord by adopting a conscious, definite, thunderously decisive act of the will. This willful attempt must be carefully balanced in the real understanding that our spirit is already victorious. All that we are really trying to do with our efforts or thoughts is to validate that which has already occurred on the cross! This then aligns the body with the reality of the spirit. Christ said it is finished and he even meant this part!

Personal peace begins with a proper perspective, how we choose to see life, and how we choose to see tribulation. This is key to stress and its management. This will be the detailed coverage of the next chapter, and possibly the most critical thought of the book.

Additionally, we need to ask ourselves is Christ first in our lives? We need to affirm the statement made by Dr. Crabbe. Luke 9:23 states, "If any man will come after me, let him deny himself, take up his cross daily, and follow me". I don't know about you, but for me, this is a very difficult verse to fulfill. What does it mean to deny oneself? What does it mean to take up his cross daily? These questions surely will not be answered here, but they do set up for us the question of where Christ is in our priorities. Personal peace comes only when we understand that we find our purpose in Him. Our purpose, when it's focused on him, dictates that we seek to minister, be good finders, seek peace, be other focused, intend to extend, and see others in the same light we want to be seen.

> *Our purpose, when its focused on Him, dictates that we seek to minister, be good finders, seek peace, be other focused, intend to extend, and see others in the same light we want to be seen.*

This does not happen as a direct result of our actions or expressed wills, but is the result of a life actively allowing the influence and "active chosen permission of the Holy Spirit" to work in our lives. It is a life that seeks relationship with Christ, the Redeemer. Yes, it is true that God's providence and will is to happen, but in our experience and peace of everyday life, our willfulness plays a valuable contribution. I have always been an overachiever, or at least an over striver, a perfectionist with a bent to never measure up!

When I realized that what I needed to do was live out his purpose for my life, and that his purpose was divinely appointed and providential, then a special feeling of relief and peace filled the corners of my soul, way down deep.

Personal peace is found when we choose to see life from God's perspective, when we choose to see tribulation or stress from God's perspective, and when we put life in God's perspective -- it's all about Him, us serving the Master, without fear, walking in the footsteps that we did not create but that He created before the beginning of time. This realization so echoes the powerful truth of Jeremiah 29:11, "God knows the plans He has for your life..." This verse combined with the understanding of Ephesians 2:8-10 which states that God ordains and causes us to walk into the works He has given us, creates a peace founded in God's power.

3. **Personal peace grows out of a proper understanding of who we were and now who we are and what we must "be"!**

Who were we? What have we become? What effect has our childhood had on forming our current understanding of who we are? Were we made or are we products of our own creation? The answers to these questions are complex but for the sake of our current understanding, all I want is for us to understand a simple yes, no, and maybe. It's not that it cannot be answered, but rather, it truly is a part of each. Are you willing to follow me on an identity pilgrimage?

Let me explain. When we were born, we were born with a nature to be self-created, self reliant, and self sufficient. We were born, and immediately, the world we lived in began the process of bending our "created ness" into the roles or positions the world around us wanted us to assume. Every family has its own dynamics and every family has its own system. When a new member enters the system, they may have desires to be "X", but there is already a powerful "X" in the family. So the process of molding begins.

I wish to call this process a moving from our "*bornness to our bentness*"; a concept I feel says it well. As we jockeyed for our emotional position, the other members of the family were working to maintain their hold on their positions. Often, the stronger personality wins and we become what others thought we were or at least what they wanted us to be, so that they felt secure in their place. So we walk through much of our lives being a "Y". For whatever reason, many of us go along with the flow. For many of us, life is spent going along to get along. Some of us challenge the system and move in to take over the "X" position and the other family member is displaced. So we live our lives not so much determined by what we wanted but by what the system bends us to be.

Life goes on until the time comes when through a tribulation, an awakening, or a move of God; we begin the process of returning to our "bornness". II Corinthians 5:17 says that we are all made new creatures in Christ. The old is gone and the new arrives. This truth is subjected to time and the realities of everyday life. We begin to realize that we are already in grace what we have not yet become in the walk of the flesh under the control of the Spirit. It is a process of becoming our true selves, thus finding personal peace in who we are and not in who we were made, by pressure, to be.

We can only grow into this peace as we work on knowing and gaining understanding into who we were made to be by the pressures of our histories. This made condition causes incongruence and much pain for the early development of our lives. Some of us might call it adolescence or, if much later, mid-life crisis. Whenever it occurs, it is the process of "bornness and bentness" finally finding peace in the genuine God created, happy little self…you!

For example, I was molded by my family to be the peace maker. I was the second-born child and I learned early in my family system that I could be funny, look to be pleasing, and the family harmony was maintained. Right or wrong, I felt loved only when I performed well and pleased my parents. Thus, the model for living a life of peace was in being a people pleasing; go along to get along person.

This set up for me a life of validating my worth through the matrix of my value being determined not by what Christ created, but rather in how I perceived others to value me! The "bentness" in my life resulted in a deep need to be pleasing, compliant, and liked. This ended and I found new insights only by deep tribulation and a "God action" that utterly transformed my image to reflect His "bornness" in me.

Jean Paul Sartre' once said, "We only become what we are by the radical and deep-seated refusal of that which others have made of us". It might also be said this way. We are what we were taught; we are what we believe; we are what we practiced; we are a collection of believed perceptions, and we are who we believe we think we are. That which we saw we learned, that which we learned we believed, that which we believed we practiced, and that which we practiced we became. We are the result of our learned past behaviors, we are the result of that which others have made us to be. Behaviors that once worked may not work now, and our hope for peace is lost. Unless this is done and the system refuses or can't change, conflict will ensue. I have heard it said, "We dislike ourselves in direct proportion to the amount of rejection and criticism we experienced in childhood." This dislike prevents our personal peace.

This rejection and criticism sets up a faulty, "stinking thinking", a way of looking at our selves through our own faults suppositions and projectors. The only way to challenge this is spiritually. Colossians 3:2 states "Set your minds on things above, not on earthly things."(NIV) Philippians 2:5 says, "Let this mind be in you that is in Christ Jesus".(NIV) We begin under this faulty system of thinking to adapt to the family motto, that is, the statement of believe that best describes your family and what they want to show the world.

In my family it was that we were Edwards' and the implication was that we were somehow inherently better. This is at least the way I saw it. This family motto created in me the need to achieve and for me that developed into the "clown", the "peace maker", the one who brought happiness to the crowd. Thus my developed and projected mask, that personification I wanted others to see, that was blocking my true self, was that of "Gospel Clown". Until I challenged these believed perceptions and this faulty sense of "bentness", I was never going to find personal peace, and neither will you. How? The answer is always going to be with an awakening to who you were created and made to be in Christ. So, we need to ask then, **who are we now**?

In 1 John 3:2 we find these words, "Dear friends, now we are children of God, and what we will be has not yet been made known. But we know that when He appears, we shall be like him, for we shall see him as he is".(NIV) What we hold in our spirits, and what we behold In Him, we become. This is a principle of seeing the realness of your "bornness" and not your "bentness". For us to move from who we were and to become who God created us to be, we simply begin to replace the old faulty thinking with the truths of God's Word.

A consistent, practiced, and applied restating begins to replace that which we thought we were with the biblical sense of who we really are. This concept is lengthy and will not be covered here. It's the process of claiming your true inheritance, your true identity, and literally transforming and renewing your mind by faithful thinking and right being. For me, the mantra or saying that began to transform my thinking was that I truly was a child of the King, A Servant of the God Most High, a friend of the Savior, anointed, cherished, elected and chosen as his adopted son.

Every time the adversary would challenge me on this thinking, I learned to fire back at him the truth found in God's Word. I would quote scripture, replace my faulty thinking with right thinking, trace the origins of this menace of disbelief, stand firm in my new belief, and eventually I would replace this old behavior or thinking with the mind of God's thinking.

Dr. David C. Needham puts it beautifully in his book, *Birthright.* "A Christian, in terms of his deepest identity, is a saint, a born child of God, a divine masterpiece, a child of light, a citizen of heaven. Not only post (usually true in the mind of God but not true in actuality here on Earth), not only judicially (a matter of God's moral bookkeeping), but actually. Becoming a Christian is not just getting something, no matter how wonderful that something may be. It is becoming someone new." (Page 47)

Who we are necessarily leads to why we are and what we are to do. The Bible tells us to enter his gates with thanksgiving and to enter his courts with praise. With a little humor, intended, I found a personal peace in becoming a "Presbybapticostalmetholuthelic" or simply stated an excited Christian, with varied denominational experiences, whose purpose was to praise the awesome God. We are here to bring honor to God. We are here to serve His desires. We are here to "posture for the pasture." We are to live under the shepherd, work with the shepherd, find our identity in the shepherd, and to become like our elder brother, the first born, the Shepherd, Jesus Christ.

We do this by speaking our expectations to God. We do this by learning to live by Gods' "Say so's ". For example, read Psalm 91: 2, it says, "I will say of the Lord, He is my refuge and my fortress, my God, in whom I trust." This says that He is my all and all and in Him I will become His all, through the finished work of Christ on the cross. It is finished, and I know why I am and what I am to do!

What I am to do, though not limited to this list, is to be responsive to Him, to be in remembrance of Him, and to be relaxed in Him. All of these R's require a willful decision to live in the reality of the new creation. Again this willful decision is couched ever so carefully in the reality of the spirit having already won and finished the battle. The willful doing is the necessary experience of the spiritual reality! We walk with Christ; we give priority to the things of the Kingdom. We actively pursue a relationship with Christ. We determine to live by faith. We count the cost. We ask the powerful question of what is our motivation to grow in discipleship, and all of this is done in us by Christ.

4. Personal Peace is sustained by practicing proper self-management

These practices of proper self-management are where we are going with the concept of *Living Up In a Down World*. The details of these thoughts are in the following chapters, here offered as a taste of the journey to come; sort of like an appetizer! If you want to manage the ups and downs of life, you must get up and get out, avoid going down and in, work out that which is within, move over and look up. This saying I first penned on a Wednesday night while I was serving a pastorate in Abita Springs, Louisiana in 1979. I have applied this rationale for recovery in almost every adventure of growth that life has dealt me. I will discuss the saying in greater detail in the section on depression; but for now suffice it to be a "mantra of worth" or a "noble sooth saying" that applies to the application of these principles.

> If you want to manage the ups and downs of life, you must get up and get out, avoid going down and in, work out that which is within, move over, and look up!

First off, do you believe in yourself? The story is told about a young elephant that was raised in a local zoo. When he was a little elephant his keeper would control him by tying him to a small stake using a 20-foot chain. During the day the little elephant would pull and tug, but to no avail. As the elephant grew older, and as time passed, he pulled, but being unable to free himself, the elephant eventually quit trying. Of course we all know what happened. The elephant not being able to free himself learned a behavior of failure and just quit trying. He no longer believed in himself. He believed his circumstances and not the truth of unlimited grace filled possibility. I ask again, do you believe in yourself or do you even like yourself? If we are going to maintain personal peace, it is essential that we believe in ourselves, our abilities, and use our strengths to the glory of God. One of my most popular versus is Philippians 4:13. It says, "I can do all things through Christ who strengthens me". So when I have the right mindset, I believe in myself, because Christ believes in me.

In the book, *I'm OK you're OK*, the author, Eric Berne, speaks of four positions or ego states that we reside in at any given point in our day or life. The positions are: I'm OK, you're OK; I'm OK, you're not OK; I'm not OK but you are OK; and I'm not OK and you're not OK. Where do you feel you live or judge yourself to be? The vast majority of us live in the" I'm not Ok but you are OK" place. This is the most common and reflects a low self-concept, which is unfortunately the place of the vast majority of Christians today, or at least this is reflectively of my twenty years plus of therapy and counseling. In answering this simple reflective question, we can begin the process of self-awareness and begin to acknowledge an area of growth in our lives.

Secondly, to maintain peace we need to put life into proper perspective and insure a proper attitude. Have I said this too frequently? I think not! This is the cornerstone of my philosophies; are we seeing the world through the worldview of Christ or are we seeing what a down world wants us to believe? When the chips are down in life, is the buffalo empty? Or, is it rather that we are facing a great opportunity for personal growth and peace. James 1:2-4 makes this critical observation. "Consider it pure joy, my brothers, whenever you face trials of many kinds, because you know that the testing of your faith develops perseverance. Perseverance must finish its work, so that you may be mature and complete, not lacking anything." A proper perspective is simply the only way we can take on the diversity of the attacks issued by the world and its ruler of darkness.

Thirdly, take each day as it comes. Learn to live in the now. Don't take yourself so seriously and learn to "jest for the fun of it". Did you know that the average five-year-old laughs 400 times a day, and the average adult laughs only eight times a day -- sad isn't it? As you take each day, one day at a time, live life with anticipation, intensity, and integrity. Never give up, predict the excellent, and live reflecting Gods "say so's".

A curious story comes to mind here that might help us internalize this concept. Some years ago I had the chance to preach in a small town called White Earth, North Dakota. It was a beautiful Sunday morning, I had never preached in a Lutheran church before, but with God's grace, I was willing. I did a service the best I knew how, shared what I felt God had given me to preach, and gave the benediction. I went to the back of the church and began to shake the hands, as is customary in most parts of the world. In just a little bit, an older lady, who was frail and a little slumped over, approached me. She clasped my hand, shook it vigorously, and said it in a loud and clear voice, "Thank you Jesus for sending him, he was fun!"

What an exciting example of living in the moment. She had little or no concern that I had never preached in the Lutheran Church, her only joy was enjoying the moment and for her that moment was exciting. She taught me a lot that day. She taught me to live in the moment, to live in the joy of the now, to worry less, and to eagerly anticipate the joys of the moment that Christ is going to bring -- for that is his nature. God is good, all the time; all the time, God is good -- for that is his nature, so I learned from some Kenyan children. Wow!

Fourthly, actively seek peace and be "other focused". Do all you can to make the most positive possible interpretation of every event that comes into your life. Believe in whose you are and to whom you serve; one who definitely placed himself behind others. Seek to find solutions rather than always looking to find out who's to blame. Learn to ask yourself," If the situation were different, or if the outcome where to be different, what would be different about me?" Develop a sense of the spiritual, which reflects an attitude of good finding. Again, seek to encourage, do little acts of unconscious kindness, do without expecting anything in return, be someone's best friend, seek to minister and to support, have a song in your heart that you sing frequently, and live like the Giffle and the Gonk.

This story of the Giffle and the Gonk is an adaptation of a Serendipity tale remembered ever so vaguely through the years. The Giffle was a tall creature and the Gonk was a little short fellow. The Giffle had long arms that stuck straight up in the air and the Gonk was flexible, but very short. The food they both enjoyed was found on a very tall tree, oh so good was this fruit; and so they both craved its yummiest flavor! The Giffle reached up and grabbed the fruit but was unable to put it into his mouth; his arms would not bend. The Gonk could not reach the fruit and was unable to get any yummiest fruit to eat. They both paused, hunger was a motivator, and they came up with this idea that would serve them both well. They both focused on the other, the Giffle grabbed the fruit, dropped it to the Gonk, and the Gonk fed them both and they lived in a state my wife calls—"preferred associates". They sought to minister, looked out for the other guy, and grew up be plump little critters who later learned to diet together, being both supportive and mutually benefiting! *Life is good with the proper sense of peace seeking and being other focused.*

Fifth, we need to live life with a view to seeing the world in a very conscious and intentional way. We can maintain our personal peace as we look at life through the "perspectives of certainties". This means living life with a plan, with the goal of being self-aware, learning to respond not react, and seeking to understand more than to be understood. The "perspective of certainties", just presented, reflects a worldview that God is providential, has not given up control, is sovereign, and is in fact looking out for our best interests.

So often, life is lived in a nonchalant, easy come easy go type fashions. We become all that we're supposed to be only by an applied conscious intentional effort. We have become accustomed to mediocrity. We often can be heard saying, "When I retire I will..." I ask the query, **why not now**? What part of the someday dream can we start living right now? Can we live selections of the dream and can we at least slow down and smell the canola? It is not so much that we do not know what to do but rather that we do not do what we already know to do! We need to concentrate and be more aware of the present and be conscious about impacting this day, not always concerned about what I might do one day.

I realize that I threw a lot of thoughts at you in a brief paragraph. The synthesis of these thoughts is that we need to practice being aware of our present feelings, thoughts, and subsequent reactions. It is my observation that we walk through life very unaware of the present. The authors of *The Blue Zone* clearly believe that we need to move naturally and more passionately. Passionate living requires active, determined, sought after, personal, in the now living!

Put a memory jog somewhere in your environment that reminds us of this truth. This could be a three by five card or a note on the refrigerator or a sticker on the front of our day timer. We can live by conscious and intentional if only we would try or think to try. On this card, state "Live in the Now". This triggers the awareness of acknowledging what you are feeling, acknowledging and processing the environment, and making choices to respond to life, and not react out of a learned, autonomic reaction.

In this process, goals for now-living emerge. It will help if our goals are both long-term and short-term, short term being this week or month and long term being in the next three to five years. They should be clearly stated, measurable, time conscience, and adaptive to time and change. Our short-term goals should match our long-term goals; they both should reflect the same direction and be complementary. Let me ask you a quick question, "what are your plans for this weekend?" Where do you hope or plan to be in the next five years. Have you shared this with your family or with other significant support systems? It is important that we keep a short-term joyful event in our futures, this helps us get through the low points in our day, keeping in mind that even short breaks can fit into the overall long-range goal; believe me this is possible and plays a significant role in maintaining our personal peace. To fail to plan is to plan to fail—and be depressed and sluggish too!

In the sections to come, there will be a great many more ideas ventured. For now, however, the last principle listed is a principle that we know so well in the north, "slow down on black ice". During hazardous driving conditions, often in North Dakota, there will be sections of the highway that are so icy and windblown that they appear dark and black. If one is not careful, and applies his brakes at the wrong time, complete loss of control might be the result. So it is that in order to maintain our peace, we need to learn to be flexible, open and always in a learning mode. Let go, go with the flow, and stop control, let God, and practice "No worries". Remember, if you do what you've always done, you will get what you've always gotten. It is a definition of insanity to expect a different outcome when we do the same thing over and over and over!

Let me close this chapter with the following wisdom question. What did the mother buffalo say to the baby buffalo the first day she left him at school? Want to guess? No! BISON!

Hope you are enjoying the book; now let us get on with *Living Up In a Down World*.

Section Two:
Principles and Concepts for Upward Living

Chapter Three:
Perspective and Attitude

Living UP in a down World is all about a strategy of learning to think accurately and appropriately about events and situations that we face each and everyday. It is learning to listen to our thoughts and examined them to see if they measure up to what God says. It is about discerning what I'm choosing to believe in; and is what I'm choosing to believe in, God's truth? Or is it a lie from the enemy? Am I practicing a very common humanistic mindset or technique of rationalization or "relativism"? I want it and that's that! Living Up is learning to deal victoriously and peacefully with situations that we can or cannot change, impact or not, depending on the permissive will of God and realizing that the victory is always found in the proper relationship to the truth of God's Word and how we applied it. Real peace is the application of all of these above statements reflected through the proper understanding of God's finished work of Grace. We are not performers of works, but professors of grace; thankful to God for the finished work of Calvary!

It is not popular to believe this today; but nonetheless, a battle for our minds is being waged all over our environment.

It is in our schools, is in our churches, is in our seminaries, and it is in all aspects that influence a life. It is subtle and crafted so well as to seem not of any concern. It is incipient and grazes just below the surface of consciousness. The battle is being waged from and for our minds. The conditioning of culture; the influence of non-Christian family/friends; the media emphasis on leisure, sex, materialism, violence, and wealth; the humanistic philosophies of, what I like to call, "me-ism" influence us. Very prevalent, and quite popular, are the aspects of spiritualism, spirituality, and the influx of pagan religions.

The very power of this tragedy is profoundly enhanced by the idea that it is not so much what the Bible says anymore, but rather what I believe and want the Bible to say concerning my "ticket punching" need or circumstance. We are more and more becoming a culture of people who want to be able to say, "God said it, I'll consider it, if it fits, then I'll believe it". It truly is not a privilege of common conversation to question popularly held concepts of acceptable behaviors; if we do, we are considered prudish or hyper religious or worse...fundamental and non progressive, judgmental and harsh! It is "progressive" to not be principled!

The Bible plainly teaches that man's feelings, passions, and behaviors are subject to and conditioned by the way he thinks. The writers of the New Testament admonish us often to have the mind of Christ and think through the matrix of the Word. In Ephesians 4, verse 23, it says: "Now your attitudes and thoughts must all be constantly changing for the better." (LB) Let's together look at several ways to keep our perspective and attitude kept on an altitude of attitude and proper belief-based perspective. A word of caution here is apt and fitting. Are we willing to learn? Can we find the motivation for change or the wants to change the way we think?

Our learning is an open and available process. Are we open and accessible to the Spirit for new leanings and new ways of thinking? Will we take the time to digest and discern the truths found and then decide to systematically apply them to our newness in Christ? Will we be like the marathon runner who has learned that he must drink well before he feels thirsty? Or will be like the proverbial prognosticator that says, "We haven't ever done it that way" or "I'll apply that truth only when it hurts bad enough!"

The reality here is that we often know what to do, but we do not do what we know to do! You see the runner has learned to relate and apply the truths now and to practice and train for the epic journey surely to come. So, I ask you to slow down, be aware of the inclination to dismiss and apply later, and to set your sails for applied and immediate action. To not be aware of our most recent inclination, that is the thought that is pervasive in our intentions, is to be unprepared and certainly fooled by the Journey's deceiver! Remember, do what you know to do and listen to what you might need to do based on new insights and gained knowledge…be a listener and a sponge. No procrastination or prognostication here, please!

A. A Proper Perspective

Look with me for a moment at the following phrase:

"OPPORTUNITYISNOWHERE"

What do you see? Look closely! Most see "opportunity is nowhere". Yet others see "opportunity is now here". In a conference I did for a neonatal ICU, one nurse found the phrase, "opportunity I snow here". She had just gone through a catastrophic winter storm.

> *The Spirit is able to do in us what we cannot do in ourselves.*

Her perspective was centered on her most recent world event. So it is true for us all. What we see in the above illustration is a reflection of our perspective in life. I believe it to be imperative that we monitor and assess our perspective in all circumstances of life. It is said that the circumstances do not make the person, but the circumstances may actually reflect who the person truly believes himself or herself to be. What is our perspective? How do we handle occurrences in life? Is our perspective a worldview or a biblical view? Let's look at our perspective. By the way, it is critical to ask the Holy Spirit for help here. The Spirit is able to do in us what we cannot do in ourselves. It is essential that we pray, "Father, show me."

Reflect with me a little bit on these following statements. Notice the difference tragically, when we have not examined our perspective or viewpoint. The world says, I'm just average, and I'm not really happy. A proper perspective says I am little less than God and crowned with glory and honor. The world says it's not my fault and I'm not responsible. A proper perspective says I am responsible. I am guilty; yet forgiven and living in the freedom of that known and confessed salvation of grace. Matthew 12:36 states, "I tell you, on the day of judgment, men will render account for every careless word they utter." Further, Romans 3:23-4 shares this, "So each of us shall give account of himself to God". The good news here is that I am redeemed and saved by the grace of God.

The world cries I'm a victim, and I've been wronged. I deserve restitution—whoa is me! The Bible teaches that you're an agent of change, salt and light, an over comer, made to be more than for yourselves, but to look out for the other and to be other focused and to look for the best in all. The world says conform, bow to "peer pressure", and try to be just like everyone else. A proper perspective, remembers that we are called to be transformed, made new, reflective of Christ, holy and separated, set apart for the work ordained for us to do. Romans 12:2 says, "Do not be conformed to this world but be transformed by the renewal of your mind, which is your reasonable service."

Culture cries out to us and demands that we expect little from life; after all, we live and then we die. We are encouraged to settle for compromise, don't rock the boat, settle in and be like the Joneses. A proper perspective, dares us to dream… to make a difference, to achieve our godly potential and to share with others the love of God. God's love applies righteousness to all; and in fact, requires godly willful obedience to the degree that we can and still live under the certainty of God's redeemed, unashamed creature that we are!

In his love, it is modeled for us to extend to others and to help them to become all that God wants them to be. My friend and coworker Mark Frueh often is heard to say, eye has not seen nor has ear heard the glories that God has in store for us. In Ephesians 3:20 we find, "Now to him who by the power at work within us is able to do far more abundantly than all that we ask or think…" Love extends and cares that others become all that they can become and so the focus is on climbing the ladder of success as partners in relationship. The

"I" meets the "I Am" and becomes the "me" working with the "Thee" to be free and become the "we."

These are just a few examples offered and statements made by the world that draws us down. In a world of improper perspective we can easily be lost and discouraged. Junk is everywhere, but God doesn't make junk. The world twists the view of faith to create chaos and loss of purpose. Furthermore, our own theologies often create a judged, guilt ridden shell of what God had intended to be a finished work of grace. We are forgiven and need to remind ourselves of this forgiveness.

> *Junk is everywhere, but God doesn't make junk!*

When we feel the need and joy of confession, thank God for the already achieved forgiveness and learn to walk in the joy of our salvation…the finished and adequate work of Christ! We have learned to accept shame as the norm.

In the premise to the book, I shared the importance of perspective. How differently it would have been had I not listened to my daughter's perspective. When she said she could not see her eyes, I could have easily judged her as attention seeking and put her to bed, later to only find her crying over wet bed sheets. The shame and the guilt I created by not seeing her perspective would have been overwhelming and useless.

This reminds me of a story about a fisherman I observed on a lake in North Dakota. Now remember, that as a storyteller, I'm allowed to exaggerate just a little bit. As a matter of fact, I remember, the daughter of one of my colleagues stepping up to me after a presentation asking me this question, "Was that story true?" No, I stated, it was just a story used to illustrate a point. In her very concrete, four-year old manner, she promptly told her mother, "Mommy, that man is a liar!" Oh well and my-my; now back to the story.

I had observed for sometime this Fisherman, catching fish and throwing away the large fish. Never having seen this phenomenon before, I waited until he came to shore and walked over and asked him why he threw away the big fish. I stated that I was from Louisiana, and we didn't throw away the big fish, we kept them and threw away the little fish. He looked at me, puzzled, and promptly stated. "You're not from around here, are you?" Possibly my southern dialect, gave me away. I told him I wasn't, but that I had an inquiring mind and the need to know. Promptly, with the forcefulness resident in the North Dakota walleye fisherman, he stated: "Around here, we throw away the big fish, because our frying pans are small". Don't you want to scream at him to buy a bigger fry pan! What a difference perspective makes. The Lord in his parables often reminds us that to hear properly and with perspective, we had to have his ears. "He who has ears let them hear!"

All through history man has struggled to have a proper perspective. Proper perspective starts with a proper source for perspective. For me, this is scripturally based sayings or proverbs. To keep my mind stayed on truth, I often quote certain sayings to remind me that truth is a perspective often found in sayings, memorable for reflection. Here are a few:

"People are not disturbed by things... but by the views which they take of them." Epictetus, 1st century AD

"I've known many troubles both big and small, but most of them never happened at all." Mark Twain

"Everything can be taken from me, but one thing! The freedom to choose my attitude and perspective in any given set of circumstances." Victor Frankl

"What lies before us, what lies behind us, pales in significance to what lies within us!" Ralph Waldo Emerson

"When you are looking at the sun, you don't see the shadows!" Helen Keller

And lastly,

"We cannot change others, others do not cause us to change, and we can only change how we perceive to think about others and about ourselves." Unknown

One last thought on perspective. Discovering proper perspective takes time. In our rapid stimulus world of smart phones and electronic constant intrusion, may I suggest this gentle insight. I notice that for many of you when you get to a red light, you gently rock your car by giving it a little gas, roll your eyes back in great despair, and blame the Department of Transportation for your being late to work. Can I suggest that we take these moments of great solitude, close our eyes and reflect on one of the statements; thusly allowing peace to settle in. Remember to keep one of your eyes, slightly opened, to avoid the certain sounds of the horn honking at you from the rear, because you appeared asleep. This will certainly destroy whatever peace you found in reflection.

B. Having a proper attitude

In almost every section of the book I have shared the importance of the concept of a proper perspective. Part and partial of this concept is the attitude we take in facing life and the contribution that attitude has for our personal peace and perspective. The question here is how do we look at life? We develop our perspective through what lens or through what filters are we consciously using to express the peace and joy of our ministries?

Critical here is the idea of being consciously aware. So much of what we do is "autonomic" or not thought through; but only a combination of hearing, practicing, believing and doing. There is a poem of sorts that teaches this notion well. "We are what we were taught, we are what we believe, we are a collection of believed perceptions, and we are who we believe we think we are. That which we saw we learned, that which we learn we believed, that which we believed we practiced, and that which we practiced we became. We are the result of our learned past behaviors, behaviors that once worked may not now work. The "systems" change; if we don't, won't, or can't change conflict in the personality ensues".

The attitude I hope to foster is an attitude of gratitude, reflective of the altitude of our belief in Christ and our belief in us as agents for God's good use. It is an attitude, that when believed, reflects "wowfulness" about the chance at life that God has given us. When was the last time you looked at your wife or at a good friend and said, "Wow, isn't she special!" This is wowfulness, an attitude that is "Up In a Down World" by choice and decision of the will; in spite of everything, it is very true that we give life the attitude we choose. It is the attitude needed to overcome the tribulations of the day, and to defeat the messages of despair that accompany life.

This attitude of up living was literally taught to me by an old friend who I remember as Aunt Maggie. Aunt Maggie was an elderly woman who lived in my first Parish in Abita Springs, Louisiana. Her daughter Mary shared that her mother was sick, and that I should visit her before too long to get to know her. Aunt Maggie had cancer! I began to develop a relationship with Aunt Maggie and over the years, we became very close. As time passed, I left the parish and went into Christian psychology. When I left, Aunt Maggie was still alive. I remember visiting her just before I took the new position,

> *It is very true that we give life the attitude we choose.*

and I was amazed that she was still active, vibrant, and very much alive. I walked into her little room that day and asked her, "Aunt Maggie, old woman, why are you still here?"

Calling her old woman was something we were accustomed to, we had become very close and this was a loving term of endearment she asked me to give her. I think of her often. She looked at me that morning; I can remember it, even as it were yesterday. She said to me, "Brother Bob, every time you visit me you say' How you doing at Maggie?' And what do I say back to you?" I paused, unable to answer, and finally told her that I didn't know. "Aunt Maggie what is it that you say?" She looked at me, with a twinkle in her eye, and it was truly a twinkle in her eye, and said, "Brother Bob, every time you ask me how I'm doing, I always say,' A little bit better!'"

I will never forget what she taught me that day. She taught me that regardless of the circumstances we could choose how we looked at them. Science has gone on to prove that a positive attitude can lengthen our lives when we have a serious illness like cancer. But Aunt Maggie didn't need to know what science had to say; she knew what life had taught her. She was the kind of woman that had such a positive outlook on life. It literally beamed through her shining eyes and she taught that to a young 31-year-old, and this young 31-year-old will never forget it. Aunt Maggie had an attitude of gratitude, she was grateful to be alive, and she practiced positive faith. She lived like our duck below!

I've had the joy over the years of many experiences like this one. I remember some years later, being asked to speak at a small church in Turtle Lake, North Dakota; home of Chaplain Curt Hansen, the man who God used to bring me to the heavenly place of North Dakota! It was about an eighty-mile drive, and on the way, I encountered very little traffic. I remember calling my father and stating that I was driving this distance and had only seen one car. He explained to me, "It must be like paradise. I'm moving there, just to avoid the crowds". He hasn't yet!

Anyway, as I was traveling down the road, I looked to the right hand side and saw an older gentleman walking back to his house, and he had a newspaper under his arm. He noticed me, probably because my car was making a great deal of noise due to the studs I had on my snow tires; I did and do live in North Dakota, you know. For no apparent reason, the older man gently turned around, using the shuffle of the elderly, and vigorously waved at me as if to say good morning. I was so struck by his greeting; I slammed on my brakes, put my red neon car in reverse, and rolled backwards to greet him as well. At which point, he once again shuffled slowly around, and vigorously waved at me, and shouted as loud as he could he shouted, "Good morning young man, 'Gooooood mooorningggg' young man!"

I was blown away. A sense of peace settled in and while taking the rest of the journey to Turtle Lake, I realized that he had demonstrated a joy that I wanted. He had no reason to greet me, he had no reason to even take the time of day to turn around and welcome me; much less share with me and greet me with a robust Good Morning! But what he taught me that day, along with Aunt Maggie, is to have an attitude of gratefulness, to have an attitude of sharing "shining eyes" with others; and in turn, blessing their lives.

God help us to be extending and gracious to all we meet. God help us to look for the best in others and to always look to minister and encourage. God help us to have this attitude about being your child, your ambassadors in life! Even as I relate this story, a sense of peace settles in over my spirit. So much a choice! There is really very little in life that we can control, but we can control our attitudes. Our stress is not often the event, but actually the way that we interpret the event and the kind of attitude and presentation of perspective we give to that event. We'll talk more about this in a moment.

As I said earlier, I find it fascinating that the world validates what in fact, the Gospel teaches us. I enjoy reading, and while I'm reading I often collect quotes and statements that seem to validate my sense of perspective. Dr. Charles Swindoll, an author I supremely enjoy, has this to say: "The longer I live, the more I realize the impact of attitude on life. Attitude, to me, is more important than facts. It is more important than the past, than education, than money, than circumstances, than failures, than successes, than what other people think or say or do. It is more important than appearance, in giftedness or skill. It will make or break a company, a church, or a whole.

The remarkable thing is we have a choice every day regarding the attitude we will embrace for that day. We cannot change the inevitable. The only thing we can do is play on the one string we have, and that is our attitude. I am convinced that life is 10% what happens to me and 90% how I react to it. And, so it is with you… we are in charge of our attitudes."

Let me share some more quotes to give you a sense of what literature and popular thought is saying through the eyes of some of its most important writers.

"Optimism, the mental habit of expecting a favorable outcome."
-- Ron L. Frank, Ph.D.

"The greatest discovery of my generation is that we can alter our lives by altering our attitudes of mind." --William Janea, Ph.D.

"We are not a wandering generality; we must be a meaningful specific!" -- Zig Ziglar

I wish to make some general thoughts about attitude, and then we'll move on to some tools we need to gain a proper perspective and a proper attitude. It is your attitude at the beginning of the task more than anything else that will determine your success or failure. The Lord reminds us in the book of Philippians that we are to have the mind of Christ and that we are to think on the things that appeared

> *It is your attitude at the beginning of the task more than anything else that will determine your success or failure.*

honest and of good report. It is your attitude towards life that will determine life's attitude towards you.

Despite many peoples belief to the contrary, life plays no favorites. The scripture reminds us that rain falls on the just and the unjust. When we can apply the biblical concept of Providence, understanding the sovereign will of God, we can walk into life with an attitude of trust and confidence. **You can control your attitude**. If you're a negative person it is because you have decided to be negative and not because of other people or circumstances.

Act as if you had a good attitude.

This decision to be negative may be the result of your "perceived and believed" histories; but at some point, we decide to stay as a negative person. It is our choice and what we need to do is ask why we do it, what we get from it, and why would we want to change?

In asking what we get from it, the concept I am getting at is that for many of us, our actins give us a secondary gain. This is a benefit that contributes to our sense of self worth and significance. For example, being depressed may get us the needed attention or sympathy. I remind you again, that circumstances do not make a person, but they simply reveal who that person believes himself or herself to be. We'll talk more about control in just a few more paragraphs.

Another general thought is this: act as if you had a good attitude. Be what you want to be! A "practiced wanted change" will eventually evolve to a "known practiced habit". Remember actions trigger feelings, just as feelings trigger actions. Before a person can achieve the kind of results he wants, he must first become that person.

For the Christian this is achieved through sanctification, a process completed at Calvary, yet experienced as daily growth. What I am sharing here is that the process of sanctification is complete; it was complete on the cross. Christ said it is finished. But in our worldview attuned to time, it is an aorist tense continually happening reality. The reason for this distinction is that if we know that we are already redeemed and we are already sanctified, the pressure of making it happen goes away and we can live in the peace of Christ's completed act.

To have a good attitude, one must then think, walk, talk, and act to conduct oneself in all affairs like the person one wishes to become. Treat everybody as the most important person in the world. (Be a good finder.) Seek to minister, doing random acts of kindness, and expecting nothing in return. Remember, attitudes are based on assumptions. In order to change attitudes, one must first change one's assumptions. This is part of the process I will later call "changing our stinking thinking"; a concept borrowed from AA. For now, act until you are!

Thirdly, develop the attitude that there are more reasons why you should succeed than reasons why you should fail. God did not make any junk. Possibly the greatest victory that the adversary has had in life, is convincing people that they are failures and there really is no reason to even try. The Eyeore syndrome, "Go ahead, it will probably fall off anyway'. When you're faced with a problem, adopt the attitude that you can and will solve it.

> *Possibly the greatest victory that the adversary has had in life is convincing people that they are failures and there really is no reason to even try.*

I can do all things through Christ Jesus, who gives me the strength. Be careful here; remember, it is not I who will solve it, but it is I with the help of the Spirit that solves problems and issues in life. Humility is all about recognizing that we are the created, and He is the Creator. It is not about us!

Fourthly, we become what we think about. Remember Proverbs tells us as a man thinks in his heart, so is he. Control your thoughts, and you will control your life. Quick thought here; we cannot control the thoughts of life-- they simply come and go. What we can control is what we do with those thoughts and what attitude and subsequent feelings will we assign to them for processing life. Radiate the attitude of confidence, of well being, of a person who knows where he is going. You will then find good things happening to you right away. Why? Because when you act confident, operating out of the mind of Christ, you defeat the "Doubter" and his deceptions.

The last point, though many more are possible, is this. In order to develop a good positive attitude, take charge first thing in the morning. Do you say, "Good morning, Lord" or "Good lord, morning?" The concept of taking charge of it in the morning means to wake up to the possibilities of "God" in control of your day. Say this each morning: "Thank you God for the beauty of the day. Walk with me as You divinely do in me what I can't do. Be my peace and guide my every step... to your glory, Amen." It really is your choice, as a matter of fact; let's go now to sharing about the concept of controlling your attitude and perspective.

C. Taking control over your attitude or perspective

Many people will say to me, "I can't help it. It is just the way I am!" Yes you can and actually you must if peace is ever going to be your destination and final station on the trip. What must first happen is for you to allow yourself the privilege of believing you do have control. Somewhere, in the impregnation of your histories, someone told you that you were just this way...settle it Robert, you are just that way. What I teach to hurters is the idea that by catching the critic (you) and correcting the thinking, you can change and take charge of your attitude. Catching the critic is catching your own self-condemnation.

Try this: say the word or make the sound of brakes stopping on an old car, "Eke Eke!" Don't laugh, say it...Eke eke! This is a way of stopping the thought process and bringing your thoughts back captive to the obedience of Christ. Now, use this formula for successfully changing a learned patterned behavior. Use the acrostic of S.T.O.P. This means to stop, think, organize your thoughts, and to proceed

S.T.O.P.
Be still,
Think,
Proceed in
Obedience,
Peace!

with peace! I have used this for years and it works. In order to take control of our attitudes and perspectives, we must confront the axioms of life that our pasts have created. Let's break it down.

The S means to stop and get still. Slow down and reprocess the thought. The Lord admonishes us to be still and know that I am God. What is said here is I am the truth and I will replace your worldly thinking if you but will slow down and pause. We don't do this often, do we? We never slow down, we seldom meditate; how sad! The Bible shares in II Corinthians 10 that we are to try and bring every thought captive to the mind of Christ. The mind of Christ is grace and peace and walking in the knowledge of our childhood and ownership by the Father.

The T means to think what and where and how this thought came to be true. It means to retrace and replace the faulty thought with a new truth; one based in your new understanding of the current living word of God. It means to think on the mind and attitude of Christ, to reframe the thought around the truths of a renewed scripture...think, think, think!

The O stands for organizing your thoughts around the truth and free. For example, I often have the thought that I am a failure or that I will never measure up. This comes from my perceptions of my childhood. I can go on believing this or I can stop and organize my thoughts around a new matrix, the matrix of value God places on me thorough the work of the Son. It means formulating a new pyramid of thought that ends up with a different conclusion or apex, a renewed and transformed conclusion.

Lastly, the P stands for the process of proceeding with peace, providence, power, purpose, and power. It is the compilation of the process that results in the new found beliefs that now replace the old corrupt thoughts. Do this time and time again, and in time, it will infect the illness of fallen man and come to be what you believe is the truth. You will have successfully changed your way of "patterned performance" and created a new schema for being. This new schema is now being filtered through the new you, the creation of the new man as reflected in II Corinthians 5:17! Remember, the Word is powerful even to the dividing asunder of the flesh from the spirit; thus, the emergence of the new man while still living in reality in the old man. The Word believed transforms!

Remember, our attitudes and perspectives on life can make the difference between coping in life or collapsing under the pressures and perceptions of life. Our faith stands equipped to turn the tide for us. So, ask the Spirit to wake up your spirits and to infuse you with the attitude of gratitude formed on an attitude of altitude, defined in the right perspective!

Chapter Four:
Tools and Strategies to develop a Proper Perspective/Attitude

A. Christian Belief System

In order for us to have the proper perspective, and for us to have the proper changing perspective and attitude, we must constantly develop a Christian belief system. A Christian belief system is one in which the word of God is used as the objective standard by which one's beliefs are measured. Very similar to what Dr. Charles Stanley said in his book, as quoted earlier in this text, are these points. A Christian belief system, says God is ever present in our lives. He is constantly

> *When we choose obedience the reward for our choices is Peace and a life of fulfillment!*

with us. He loves us and has the very best intentions for us. He is our Father, loving, and yet righteous, expecting obedience, yet graceful enough to cover our disobedience with the cross. When we choose obedience, the reward for our choices is Peace and a life of fulfillment! The joy of the pattering puppy feet! Thanks David and Pat!

Let me say a few words of clarification here. This developed system or belief system does not create peace. This system maintains and sustains a close relationship with Christ necessary for our grace"fully" given lives to be full of current experienced joy. What I am saying is that grace is a finished act and the sustaining and the ability to enjoy the journey is not in our acts of performance but in the given finished acts of Chris and the grace of God! I hope this helps with condemnation and performance anxieties! This is critical: systems or lists of "keys to" do not create peace, they sustain the gift of peace God gave us in His Son!

A Christian beliefs system believes in repentance and recognizes that our beliefs are constantly being transformed and renewed. This repentance should not create a wealth of guilt. The proper response of repentance is to thank God for the gift of His son and to then desire and return to the fellowship of the relationship with Christ, doing so as a child not scolded, but affirmed and loved unconditionally!

We need always to allow Christ to shape our thoughts into His thoughts; after all, His thoughts are higher than our thoughts. It is difficult work to interpret the influences of changing culture and updated information from good science. One only needs to consider the role of the sexes or the role of music in our worship and culture. It is hard to change and it is even harder to discern whether God is in it or not! The ability to shape our thoughts takes time, scripture, and obedience.

A Christian belief system sees things from God's point of view. Our worldview will influence everything we think, feel, or act on because it is the foundation of our "rationally thinking" American culture. We process life through our intellect and not our emotions. A belief system that is biblical in rational intellectual, and processes through our minds. It is, I believe, the basis of much of Scripture.

Potentially, the greatest danger here is that of the concept of the "Great I Am versus the Great I can". This is basically the idea that man is all about himself. This perception and attitude always leads to destruction, though it is absolutely the mantra and motto of this age. Rick Warren opens his book *The Purpose Driven Life* with the idea that it is not about us, it is all about the glory of God. So basic, yet, it impacted our culture like sliced bread and the television did in our recent past. Is our point of view God's point of view? We could begin each day asking the Holy Spirit to reflect so strongly through our lives that we see and think through Him. Again, fear is that our thoughts could be self-generated and not Spirit generated.

Just a few quick thoughts of clarification here might be in order. I share these few thoughts to help you process the importance of your worldview. Our overall worldview on life must reflect the grace based perspective of God in the new covenant. We are no longer under the Law, yet our guilt often places us under the harsh need to perform. Let us remember Romans 8:1 where it is clear that there is no condemnation for those called to the purpose of God! If you will take a close look at these few thoughts, I believe it will begin to give you a little of the way in which I have come to know the emerging Peace God promised.

Now four questions with little explanation needed at this time. Can we own that we are God's Choice? Can we admit that we are addicted to alien god's, god's of our own creation coming out of the need to self medicate, pacify our pain reduction; i.e., food, alcohol, sports, RV's, cabins, and money! Can we confess and acknowledge our God defiance and reclaim an intentional God reliance? Lastly, can we repent in order to replenish? This meaning that when we repent it is the reestablishment of the unscathed image Christ has for us through the cross!

Additionally, a Christian belief system has a commitment to believing God's truth rather than Satan's lies. John 10:10 says that Christ came so that we might have life and have it abundantly. A large portion of abundant living, or living up in a down world, is saying yes to God's truth and no to Satan's lies. This belief system also acknowledges that what God says about us is the truest way to receive our self-concept. God has much to say about us as humans, but so does the world.

The world teaches a belief system of self-destruction, couched carefully in the mantle of success and riches gained. After all, the one who dies with the most toys wins! It is irrational, misinformation, and comes from the thinking of a faulty fallen world. Moreover, the Christian belief system takes the Bible as God's authority for life. A redeemed Christian calls certain behavior sinful on the authority of God's Word, ever debating the impact and synthesis of new thinking; but ultimately, relying on God's Word to set us free from rationalized behavior.

> *A large portion of abundant living is saying yes to God's truth and no to Satan's lies.*

A Christian belief system finally, but not conclusively, recognizes that the implementation of new insights, renewing the mind, and changing behavior needs to come from the power of the Holy Spirit. This I believe is consummately the most trying of the aspects of a Christian belief system. The constant influx of new thought, new revelations, new theologies, all proposing to be based in progressive and upward thinking and each needing new reevaluations. It is a liberation type theology that is hard to reconcile against the traditionally and borne theology we grew up with.

I wish to thank the authors of the text, *Rational Christian Thinking*, for the bulk of these thoughts, each of which forms the basic views of "Living Up". The parallels are distinctly biblically and I found the thoughts ever so helpful in forming my constructs for the text and philosophy of "Living Up".

In today's culture, it is very difficult to practice a right thinking combined with a right believing. This little story should illustrate this and form a basis to "jump or leap" to our next thought, a pun intended! A group of frogs were traveling through the woods, and two of them fell into a deep pit. All the other frogs gathered around the pit. When they saw how deep the pit was, they told the unfortunate frogs they would never get out. The two frogs ignored the comments and tried to jump up out of the pit. The other frogs kept telling them to stop because they were as good as dead. Finally, one of the frogs took heed to what the other frogs were saying and simply gave up. He fell down and died. The other frog continued to jump as hard as he could. Once again, the crowd of frogs yelled at him to stop the pain and suffering and just die. He jumped even harder, and finally made it out. When he got out, the other frogs asked him, "Why did you continue jumping? Didn't you hear us?" "Hear what?" The frog explained to them that he was almost deaf -- he thought they were encouraging him the entire time!

This is the framework for the concepts of being up in a down world. On the radio broadcast that I do two days a week, it is the basis of the broadcast that I will present sound biblical concepts couched in good psychological understanding to answer the difficult questions of today. Not psychobabble, but psychological constructs subjected to the scrutiny of Scripture. This is exactly what we are going to do now, present concepts for living positively in this complex and evolving age. Let us go and eat some grass for the hopper! By the way, don't stay up later than you should, we can journey some more another day!

B. A Tool of Proper Worldview

What is our view on life? How do we see the world? Is it a biblical worldview based in the concept that it is all about Him? What is your life motto or what is the metaphor we base our life journey on? Does it for you, like a race, need to be a life where we can be the victors all the time. Could your life motto be like that of a merry-go-round, constantly spinning with no base and no ultimate victory, always expecting a surprise around the turn of next bend? Is it like a circus, crazy with three rings, going all the time; a life of multitasking, with no sincere and genuinely singular purpose for your life? This is probably the most popular model for me. It was said by one of my earliest professor, Dr. Carroll Freeman, that life was like a man with 10 fingers pointed in ten directions, and that what I need to do was to find a distinct and clear meaning, to focus those fingers into a more pointed direction. I learned this to be true only in my fifties; sorry Dr. Freeman for the delay. Could our life motto be that of a battleground, a world where the game was most important and taking casualties was part of the necessary consequences of winning the war? For my close friends Mark Frueh and Steve Oster, it is best described as a life for the adventurer. A life where each is set out on a journey to discover new truths like a discoverer finds new treasure. For them, it is a journey of new insights created by the filling and renewal of the mind, each day a new adventure in learning and applying God's word.

I fear that for much of this generation, the life motto might be "Cry Baby, suck your thumb" or "The most toys wins". Caution here; our generation had its problems and we need not cast too deep a shadow on this generation, for they are a product of our own allowed deceptions. This is the life view or motto that says all of life is about what I want and what I can get is mine and mine only. It appears to be a generation with the motto or life metaphor of narcissism (meism). Let me be careful here in not expressing that this is all that this generation is about. There are very bright lights in and on the horizon, but it is clear to me that the pervasive metaphor is that of my getting ahead soon, by thirty-five, and at almost any cost. This reflects in the statistics of couples not marrying and a couple choosing not to have

> *We are to store up riches and treasures for the life to come, not in this "rented space" we call earth; in the end, we are just renters of this temporal guesthouse.*

children because they get in the way of success and upward mobility. A worldview where I am in charge and everything is relative to what I want and think rather than on an objective standard for measurement. The world is subjective and relative to my needs and wants and desires.

For instance, let's create for ourselves a worship service that meets the needs of our generation of technology and entertainment. When we leave the service we ask the necessary questions as to whether or not we left entertained and did the speaker challenge us with witty and humorous anecdotal comments. Worship for this mindset is all about being sensually titillated and then going out to lunch and discussing the merits of the music and the speaker's relative ability to keep the congregation engaged and "entertained". It is as if we could charge admission and have each of us purchase a ticket, and if the show was not good we could simply not purchase another ticket next week and stay home. Tickets please! Harsh, maybe; reality, yours to decide! Couldn't we just as well reflect on how the thoughts of the worship collated with our weeks devotions and how did the worship enhance our own private daily worship joys and experiences? Could we ask, "Did we train as hard to hear the praise and applications of the service as the worship leaders worked to present a declaration from God?" Did our worship bring honor to God? Could we somehow take the focus off of us and put it on Him and make an us and You out of our worship.

In order for the concepts presented in this book to work, it is going to be imperative that we follow after the teachings of Matthew 6:21, in that, we are in this world to bring glory to and worship for the Lord. We are to store up riches and treasures for the life to come, not in this "rented space" we call earth; in the end, we are just renters of this temporal guesthouse. Our heart must be trained to prepare ourselves to accept and appreciate that it is all about God and it is all about His glory. God created us for His good pleasure and not for us to gain our good pleasure at the expense of His glory and worship.

When I wake each morning, I say a statement in prayer that goes something like this: "Dear Lord, thank you for the beauty of the day. Thank you Lord that all that happens to me is in your plan and providence and that I will be doing what you have already planned for me to do. Thank you that I do not have to worry or be concerned about the future, that I can live in the day, and that you have the joy of my walk as your primary concern. You have dispatched angels to care for me and that care is ultimate and certain. Thank you that what I get done today is what you had in mind and what I do not get done is for tomorrow. Help me to discern the difference between my wants and desires and your will and purposes. Lord, walk with me today…Amen and Amen!"

A Christian belief system and a proper biblical worldview are created, not out of the natural, but by the molding of the mind. This molding is not easy. Quite frankly, it is down right difficult. For many, me included, being molded means work, devotion, some sacrifice, and a movement toward the stillness of God. For this, I refer you to the book by Dan Wolpert entitled, *Creating a Life with God*. So, a key tool for a worldview is to keep worship in the place of bringing glory to God. This tool will help us to not fall into the trap of entertainment and light hearted addressee of worship. This is enough for now.

C. Strategic Identity Awareness: Again who are we and to whom do we belong

Strategies are determined, rehearsed, and carefully thought out schemes to make life work. So far we have discussed two: a Christian belief system and a proper worldview. The matrix of a prevailing view of Christian values being applied to a worldview that says, "When in doubt go with the Word." We must constantly be vigilant in checking the "critic" (us) and reframing our thinking. Now let's turn to strategy number three: strategic identity awareness (knowing who we are).

To discover the concept here, let's look at the most astonishing prayer I believe to be found in the New Testament, that of Ephesians 3:14-21. It states, "For this reason, I kneel before the Father, from whom his whole family in heaven and on earth derives its name. I pray that out of His glorious riches, He may strengthen you with power through his Spirit in your inner being, so that Christ may dwell in your hearts through faith. And I pray that you, being rooted and established in love, may have power, together with all the saints, to grasp how wide and long and high and deep is the love of Christ, and to know this love that surpasses knowledge -- that you may be filled to the measure of all the fullness of God. Not to him who is able to do immeasurably more than all we ask or imagine, according to his power that is at work within us, to him be glory in the church and in Christ Jesus throughout all generations, forever and ever! Amen." (NIV) Can you imagine any better definition of the life that God intended for our strategic identity to be made known and available to His deployment and victory! Let's break it down bit.

First off, in the section on personal peace we stated that *it behooves us to be certain that we know who we are.* Paul begins his prayer with a solid awareness of our truest self-identity, "in your inner being," that deepest realm of human personhood, which will someday grace heaven itself and which alone, is equipped by God to express authentic meaning in life. It is an awareness of one's identity and meaning in life. We must, at some point, take a strong moral and spiritual inventory of ourselves and who we really are!

Recently, a study was performed by Ted Stossel of CBS news, stating the five fundamental aspects of peace, or to put it another way, keys to happiness. He states that one of the five fundamental concepts of happiness must be that we have found a meaningful and purposeful life. He had no interest in being biblical, but he does point up the biblical truth, and that, purpose and meaning must be found in the procured and impugned use of God's gift gifting. The Blue Zone group study also lists the "development of a spiritual identity" as critical to overall health. That is to say, God gave us each a purpose which we must obtain by insights, study, prayer, and a desired application of what this search reveals.

Strategically, our identities are found, fulfilled and completed in the discovery and usage of our individual gifts and the ministry that this knowledge then produces. The Christian who wants to live up cannot be like a sponge that is never wrung out and it is allowed to dry out and decay. Rather, no greater joy is found than in the discovery and usage of one's Ministry designed to help others. For it is in the concept of being "other focused" that we find our deepest identities.

Secondly, *strategic identity must be located in the unconditional issue of the Lordship of Christ*. We must be like Thomas. When confronted by the authenticity and confidence of the cross and with the evidence of what Christ did, he proclaimed to the world, "My Lord and my God". Timothy relates the world of the "horizontal" to the world of God, the "vertical". It is to say, as Steve Oster says, "Go vertical!" Thanks Steve for this powerful thought and mental image of our faith!

Paul states in his prayer that we must have an absolute submission to the Father, "I kneel before the Father." He then

(Go Vertical!)

concludes his prayer with absolute commitment to the glory of God, "To Him be the glory!" In order for strategic identity to be understood and for the goal of personal peace to be ours in an up world, we must examine carefully where we have allowed our lives to be about ourselves, which is the natural inclination of our humanity, and not to be about the glory of God. Does Christ dwell in our hearts? Interestingly, the word Paul chooses for "dwell" literally means, "to be at home in." In other words, there can be no proper perspective until Christ is truly "at home" in your life. Well, what a difficult concept, Lordship. It certainly will take the next strategic placement for us to achieve this lofty and hoped for identity.

Thirdly, let's work on coming to the understanding that we modern self-sufficient Christians *often negate or minimize the impact and power of the Holy Spirit*. We either see it as an emotional experience that is well overplayed, or in our own self-sufficiency, we don't give permission for the spirit to impact our conceptual "wheels for going about life". What I mean by this, is that in order for us to be strategically ready to live up in a down world, we must allow the "willful resolution" to invite the Holy Spirit into our lives so that He is a power that might be operative.

This is to say, that God, or at least it is my understanding, allows us the privilege of choice. We can choose to invite and welcome the presence of the Holy Spirit, or we can, by the act of omission, go about our daily lives; resting only in our cognitive and rational skills. Plainly stated, the Holy Spirit is a presence and power that must be an experienced reality. "Strengthen you with power through his Spirit".

Could that possibly be non-experiential? I don't think so; as a matter of fact, it's plain to my experience, it is just can't happen. Why? Because when we allow the presence of that power, it will produce in you, spiritual comprehension with dimensions beyond your dreams. This then becomes an awareness of the love of Christ, which surpasses knowledge. This is the understanding of John 14:26 where it states; we shall have a peace that surpasses our wildest understandings and cannot be created by our own comprehensions. "Over comer", invite the spirit to do its work, do it often, do it willingly, and do it now! This is a conscious and intentional act of the will done moment by moment and day by day. Ask the Holy Spirit to reveal in you right now how it is you are allowing His powerful and awesome work in your mind and heart!

Fourthly, this is admittedly, one of the author's personal pet peeves. The Barna Institute, which is a group that studies trends in modern Christianity, reports that in 1963, 94% of Christians attended church worship on a regular basis. In 2002, this number has dropped to 24%. Astonishing might be good term to use right now. It appears that for the pursuit of personal happiness, the admonishment of Hebrews 10: 24 through 26 have been circumvented by the need or justification for an "Isolated Pilgrimage". *Body life participation is a prerequisite for living up in a down world.* It is not that we "go to church", but rather that we "belong to church".

Paul states in these verses, "being rooted and established in love, may have power, together with all the Saints… to him be glory in the church." If this were not enough, the next three chapters that flow out of his prayer are packed with relational issues with love at the center. Remember, the greatest need that we have is "relational authenticity". We want to belong and have what we belong to be real and viable. This is a highly debated and controversial subject. I do not pretend to express the absolute truths, but only what works for me. I believe that we can worship God in isolation, but it will not be the best worship that God has in mind for us. The best is family, the family of the church.

From history, we draw the fact that from the daily life of the early Christians came a pattern worthy of emulation by Christians of every generation: "They met constantly to hear the apostles teach, and to share the common life, to break bread, and to pray. With one mind, they kept up their daily attendance at the temple, and, breaking bread in private houses, shared their meals with unaffected joy, as they praised God and enjoyed the favor of the whole people" (Acts 2:42, 46 -47, NEB). So comprehensive an expression of fellowship and faith is this, that it makes the halfhearted witness of men in our day seem pale. They often tend to limit their spiritual concerns to the 11 o'clock hour on Sundays.

What about the life of Christ? Let us draw something from the life of Jesus himself. Joseph and Mary, having lost track of Jesus in Jerusalem, wondered where they might find him. He was in the place, which was most congenial to his nature. In the temple he was speaking with a learned man, for they were the keepers of his Father's house. Even as a child Christ recognize the need and place of gathering together for the work of the Kingdom. Further, Paul writes in Philippians 3:20 that we are a colony of heaven. Each church is a frontier settlement in the divine expansion, which shall continue until Jesus' return. Wherever the sun does his excessive journeys run, there shall the church collected be found!

Talk with you about this for a second...seriously! If all we know is contained within what we've experienced, all our future decisions will be based entirely on the information that we know. This then sets up for us a closed system of perception and actuality. The isolation that we choose for worship does not allow us to be pollinated, and all the conclusions we draw about life are never challenged. Sure we can worship God at the lake, sure we can worship God in our cabin setting; but we need to hear the thoughts of other Christians so that our worldview can be impacted by what the Spirit provides in our corporate worship and identity. We need "other" to be challenged. We need "other" to be validated and affirmed. We need "other" to express our ministry gifts; plainly, we need "other". Besides, when we ignore or replace the congregation with other support systems, we cheat our family. They need us to be part; maybe the very part or encouragement that is supplied uniquely only by you.

God made us in His own image and this includes the need for "other". Sociologists tell us that we need upwards of six support systems in our lives to be healthy. The church is one of these vital support systems. I believe it to be strategic and necessary that we participate in the body life of the Church. Christ calls us to the relational experience. Do with this what you may, but I guarantee that when you give the "old hypocrite" of the church a chance, God will pay healthy and hefty dividends, for that is his nature.

Now let's consider what it is that might be stopping our participation: injury, an angry moment, a mistreatment, an injustice, all of these legitimate and strong reasons to afford further pain. It is my prayer that through reconciliation these injuries can be healed. We need each other and we need the community of a gathered operating ministry team, and sadly as it might seem to many, the church is that ordained place to feed and nourish the mind of the Christian, young and old. Enough!

Lastly, let us look at the *strategic need for the submitted will*. In the model prayer, Christ teaches us to say, "Thy

Kingdom come, Thy will be done". Holiness demands the active participation of the will. Recall that we earlier shared that we needed to bend our will to that of the Master for peace to result. This was by necessity an act of "conscious intentionality". This "bentnees to bornness" conscious return is brought about by the necessity of the submitted will of man, driven by the divine devices of the Holy Spirit! Fundamental in this prayer is the ardent fervor in which Paul is doing the asking. Not only for others, but certainly we should assume for himself also. One more word in this prayer spotlights the will. It is the word "faith". Faith is the expression of the willing will to ascend to the truth of God's word. There can be no peace without the exercise of the will in favor of faith and grace.

A.W. Tozer is admittedly one of my favorite writers. In his books, one of his overarching thoughts is that "modern man" has substituted the easy for the required. God requires His church to gather. The easy road is often taken today. It is to accept the gift of salvation without any absorption of sacrifice. Tozer states with emphasis, "The church is the most vital of all institutions—the only one that can claim a heavenly realm of origin." This found in *God Tells the Man who cares*, pg.64.

According to scripture the church is the habitation of God through the Spirit. The church, the influence if the body life, is pivotal in a well rounded, developed strategy that affirms our identity. We need the constant, positive reinforcement of exhortation given by and within the walls of the church. If we think not, I abhor you to examine why not, correct it, ask why, and go on! The model to the world and to the generations to come is definitely strategic…we need each other.

D. Spiritual Growth Tools

In very many instances, I find fault in teachers when they do not do enough to tell us the how of their perspective or teach us the way to their beliefs. To develop the perspective needed to be up, one needs the fundamental sense of a basics course on spiritual tools for growth. This list is brief and in no way exhaustive, but serves only to accentuate the need for the basics of discipleship. To find perspective and attitude these skills are developmentally necessary. These texts are taken from the NIV version of the Bible.

1. **Bible study-- "Study to show yourself approved by God, a workman who does not need to be ashamed, rightly handling the word of truth". 2 Timothy 2:15**

2. **Prayer--"Don't worry about anything, but take every little detail to the Lord in earnest in thankful prayer and the peace of God which passes all understanding shall keep your heart at rest in God". Philippians 4:6-7**

3. **Fellowship—"And day by day they continued in one mind in the temple, and breaking bread from house to house, they were taking their meals together with gladness and sincerity of heart." Acts 2:46**

4. **Discipleship—"Let the word of God dwell richly in you with all wisdom, teaching and admonishing one another with psalms, hymns and spiritual songs, singing with thankfulness in your hearts to God". Colossians 3: 16**

5. **Stewardship—"For I testify that according to their ability, and beyond their ability, they gave up their own accord, begging us with much fervor for the favor of participation in the support of the Saints". 2 Corinthians 8:3 –4**

6. **Service and Ministry gifts—"As each one has received a special gift, employee it in serving one another as good stewards of the manifold grace of God". 1 Peter 4:10**

7. **Repentance—And Peter said to them, "Repent, and let each one of you be baptized in the name of Jesus Christ for the forgiveness of sins; and you shall receive the gift of the Holy Spirit." Acts 2:38**

8. **Practicing Christ-likeness—"For by these He has granted us His precious and magnificent promises in order that by them, you may become partakers of His divine nature, having escaped the corruption that is in the world by lust." 2 Peter 1:4**

This list is by no means and cannot certainly be exhaustive. Hidden within these strategies is the concept of drinking before you're thirsty. What I mean by this is simply *that we cannot have the proper perspective unless we have the disciplines before the situations occur.* I know of a delightful woman, an ex-police officer, Family Nurse Practitioner, dynamic and self-contained. When she is stressed out, I offer the suggestion that she take a deep and slow breath. Whereupon, she takes a rapidly shallow breathe. I laugh…she hits me and life goes on. Seriously, before I loose this friendship, what I am sharing here is the need to prepare through the disciplines of spiritual growth before the need arises.

I'm afraid that today we're a lot like the story of the grasshopper and the ant. In the story, the ant prepares for the future, stockpiling his resources and investing well. The grasshopper does what the grasshopper always has done, works some, invests little, and waits on Social Security and retirement. In the end, grasshopper finds little preparation and did not learn to drink before he was thirsty. Remember the Olympic runner? The runner would never have made the race if they had not learned the discipline of drinking before they were thirsty. Well before the race was over, and well before the body told them they were thirsty, dehydration will set in, the muscles stiffen and the race would come to an end.

Preparing for daily life needs the disciplined approach of an athlete. We may not be marathon runners but we each are determined to lack peace if we lack a discipline of sacrifice… ask God to illumine and grant this gift to you.

E. Stopping Stinking Thinking: "Catching the Critic"

Peter Eide, a popular Christian rapper, was reported to have said this: "It is not that my glass is half full or half empty; but the fact that I have a glass at all is awesome!" What a perspective balanced in the truth of God's reality. It is not so much our circumstances that matter, but that God is in those circumstances.

> *We need to plant the truth, applying the constant and repetitive relevance of this truth, so that we might replace and erase that which we have learned by faulty thinking.*

What a fantastically positive way to look at life. Certainly, one of the keys to living up in a down world is that our truth for thinking must process itself through Proverbs 23:7, which once again says, "As a man thinks his heart so is he". What this is saying is that we need to learn to inspect what we expect; we need to learn to inspect, carefully consider the source, and then prayerfully perceive what we expect God wants us to do.

This is accomplished by the careful inspection of what we're basing our lives on. If we're basing our lives on the common worldview, then we're basing our lives on something that's going to change and fluctuate with time and with the circumstances. Our goal might be to learn to think through the matrix of Christ, to bring life issues through Christ and not to bring life issues through our troubled world mindset. Again, this could be called spiritual warfare, or as I have liked to call it "scriptural warfare".

How do we see the truth? We process truth through what we believe to be true; our perceptions flow through our "collected believed perceptions"; truth is not relative; if we think so then our thinking is, in my opinion, perverted. For the Christian, we need to consistently inspect the filter that we're running our thoughts through. Is that the mind of Christ or is it based rather on our fears and worries of the moment? A.W.Tozer writes exhaustively about the need to think right. I commend the reading of his book *Born after Midnight*. He makes several stromg points supporting "as a man thinks in his heart so is he".

Thinking stirs feelings and feelimgs bigger action. Our volunteer thoughts not only reveal what we are. They predict what we will become. By using Holy Spirit inspired thinking, we and help our minds be pure sanctuaries in which God will be pleased to dwell. The habit of holy thinking is a long and needed practice. For more, I hope you might pick up and read his essays...powerfull!

It tells us in Psalm 119:89 that the Word of God is forever, eternal, standing firm in the Heavens. This then becomes our compass point, our stable point, and our rock that we can rest on. Joshua 1:8 tells us to be strong, be strong in the book of the Law. We are to keep the strong word within us. And this then becomes the basis for our thinking.

Notice what it tells us in James Chapter 1, versus 21 through 25: "Therefore, get rid of all moral filth and the evil that is so prevalent and humbly accept the *word planted in you*, which can save you. Do not merely listen to the word, and so deceive yourselves. Do what it says. Anyone who listens to the word, but does not do what it says is like a man who looks at his face in the mirror and after looking at himself, goes away in immediately forgets what he looks like. But the man who looks intently into the perfect law that gives freedom, and continues to do this, not forgetting what he has heard, but doing it -- he will be blessed in what he does." (NIV)

I placed italics on the words planted in you, because this is the application of the word that should be our guide. We need to plant the truth, applying the constant and repetitive relevance of this truth, so that we might replace and erase that which we have learned to be faulty thinking. Again, insights gained create the opportunity for personal choices to change, but often, we do not choose because of secondary gains. Secondary gains might be the notion of resident sin or comfortable sin, keeping us from peace and upward living. These are powerful and often considered strongholds, needful of special attention. The careful work of a partner or therapist can help. Always be open to help, it is patterned after the Master!

Let's look at this faulty thinking just for a second. Let's call these faulty thinking "myths and misbelieves", strong words because they need to be. Myths often become truth by fanciful thinking and inadequate inspection of what's being said. Misbelieves are lies people tell themselves about themselves, circumstances or others. Sadly, the author of these myths and misbelieves is the critic, and the critic is "us". Let's illustrated this in the following way, OK!

Our minds are like fertile fields or gardens, if we plant and water with distress, we get weeds of distress. But when we use proper fertilizer, plant with good seed, and water with the concepts of peace and the scripture, we grow a fresh and renewed crop. Unfortunately we often use too much water from the world and our relativity produces a worldview that pervades over our biblical view. I've said this before, but it's important. We are responsible to manage our lives and the word gives us the strength to be "Response-able".

We can be responsible in the handling of the Word and the Word will make us response able in the world! The practice of worship, fellowship, prayer, and Bible study will create in us the ability to defend our hope (I Peter 3:15). The belief in the book of beliefs helps us to investigate, give an accurate account, and then apply the truth to these circumstances. It's important to note that we need to take action. We need to take action by recognizing some of the habits of distorted thinking.

In modern psychology, I have seen lists, as long as 12, but for this instance, I want to talk about only a few. There's a distorted thought of selective abstraction. What this means is that we focus only on certain details from the complex picture. We don't see the big picture, but only the fear that sits in front of us. We want what we want. We rationalize the command, decide to have it our way, and selectively base our lives on what I want the text to say. Arbitrary interference is another distorted thinking concept. This is where we draw conclusions without evidence or in the face of the evidence we draw anxious conclusions. The word arbitrary implies our being the arbitrator, the fulcrum, the pivotal point of decision being housed in me-me-me! The end is justifying the means; after all, God wants me to prosper. The conclusion drawn is biased by a strong conclusion that grace allows or permits, even promoted, a lack of obedience and sacrifice. For example, ask yourself this question, why does it take us so long to open up an envelope from the I.R.S.? We assume, based on inadequate information, that we're being audited. Truth hurts doesn't it!

Then there's the distorted thinking, called over generalization. This is when we draw a conclusion on the basis of a single incident. We need to be careful about the words, everyone, no one, everything, always, and never. "I'll always be a failure; nothing ever goes right; everything in my life stinks; and I'm just a loser." By far, the worst two distortions are personalization and magnification. In personalization, it means that we are relating events to oneself fault without evidence that they are even related. Let me give you an example. We pass someone in the grocery store and we say hello. They don't speak. We immediately assume we've offended them and that something's wrong based on something we've done to them. We don't stop to ask ourselves, are they having a bad day; but rather we blame ourselves, this is called personalization and it is a wicked tool of the adversary. This then creates a personal self-concept, a projective personality that ends up apologizing all the time or saying "I'm sorry" all the time. I want to ask that person how sorry are they, 100% sorry or just 50% sorry. The point is that we are not "sorry"; what we did may have been a sorry thing to do, but we are not sorry. God did not make junk!

Magnification is the simple process of over emphasizing a negative aspect of the situation. It can also be called "catastrophizing" or building a mountain out of a molehill. This too is a very common distortion, often used to "awfulize" a situation. I remember when my wife shared with me we were going to have twins. And I was 50 years old. I panicked and all I could see was how was I going to pay for the expense of two children in college at the same time. I did not stop and consult the provision of the Lord and for almost 3 weeks I was scared to death that I was going to fail. And I did not believe that God could be my provision. This is an excellent example of magnification and resulted in a great deal of distress. The action of applying the Word stops the incubation of fear. This allows our thoughts not to percolate as long, thus not building a stronghold or tower, useful to the mind of deception. Being aware of these distortions and looking out for them can be helpful. The tool that helped me to stop all of these distortions is "ABCD".

Let's make one more strong biblical point before we look at the final concept associated with the ABC Diagram. In Matthew 7:24 and following we have the story of a house built on the rock. He states that whoever hears the words and put them into practice is like a wise man that's built his house on the rock. Notice the clear emphasis here on the word being implanted. The point being that the storms of life are going to come. We can either retreat to the storm shelter, or we can retreat to the "difference maker". The question becomes how do we build a house? Have we taken the time to carefully examine the foundation, asking the question is this foundation accurate? Or is it the result of some trouble in my past. Have we been careful not to eclipse God, are we a people of sand resting hope on our own resources and not God's provision. The world is passing away. What man would invest in a failing business venture? The world is passing away. Store no treasures here on earth where the moth and corruption can ruin. Let the tension in your shoulders release, God is on the throne, his rule is secure, and we can rest in this. Not rest and say "Oh well", but rest in the overall sense of God's care and providential care being the way it is! Aah! Deep breathe! Let's look at ABCD.

Simply put, take an event in your life (a), interpreted through the word of God (b), and the end result will be a proper interpretation of the event (c). If not, a (d) will result and confusion and distress emerges. We need our vitamin (b)! Now, how do we build the reservoirs of vitamin (b)? We need to acknowledge the truth that we have these misbelieves. We need to locate our misbelieves. We need to own them, and process new beliefs. This is a simple process of cognitive reconstruction. Some examples might be; I'll never measure up, my sister is smarter (she is), I must get good grades, I'll never amount to anything, or I must be beautiful and wealthy to be accepted. Remember, it is not what happens to you in life, but how you interpreted it, and what you have allowed yourself to believe about it. Nobody but you has the power to make you miserable. I never liked that saying either, but in truth, it is correct. You can't make me mad; I choose to react to you in a mad way. It is helpful to look into the past to understand the present. Do not abide in the rooms of stinking thinking.

We need to spend time in the word. Allowing the Holy Spirit to lead us is critical. We need to remember the concept of social supports and having people in our lives that we allow to speak frankly and openly to us. We need to allow others to point out our misbelieves. We need to act by removing the incorrect belief. This is an act of the will, a want to return to whom Christ made us in our "bornness" (2 Corinthians 5:17). We need to replace the disbelief with truth by often and continually replacing it with the truth, this then , displacing our old thinking, and eventually replacing the old misbelieves with a new image from Christ. We need to expect to reinforce and reinforce and reinforce this concept many times.

This is an event of all things becoming new, a process of sanctification or event. Sanctification is an accomplished event at Calvary; however, it is important at this point to note that it is part of our "effective experience" that matters. We feel a process of sanctification, when in God's already realized reality; it is so at the Cross. A careful look at Ephesians presents this concept of a walk in grace. It is indeed finished!

Let me share a personal story from my past. I appreciate your attention, and I believe this may be the most important story that my life has known. In 1987, I was admitted to a psychiatric hospital with a diagnosis of a deep depression. I felt suicidal, sad, all alone, and rejected by God. The circumstances in my life had become overwhelming. I didn't know which way was up and all I could think was that I was once again a failure and death would be an option. They diagnosed me as codependent, a term not found in the manuals but made popular by the recovery movement. The term codependent simply means that you allow someone else to have the power to control how you feel about yourself. Your worth is always found in someone else and not within yourself. I later realized that this was in fact true, but in my despondency, I felt unloved and once again, it was my entire fault. To no one's fault, I felt like a flat river worm from Mississippi or lower Louisiana. I felt unloved and unlovable, and

I needed help. There was an emptiness feeling in my chest the size of a grapefruit and it ached all the time.

This is my own personal journey, my own personal experience; and it is certainly open to your scrutiny, but it doesn't change what happened for me. I dreamed that night that I was wrestling with an angel. I remember hearing the angel tell me that God loved me, just as I was and that I didn't need to perform anymore. His grace was sufficient to cover my pain. He loved me so much that performance did not matter. I had done a good job and I was always a good boy because I was His adopted chosen son. I had never felt adequate, even after many successes in life. But praise to God, on that night, I heard the word of the Lord and realized who I really was, a loved child of my heavenly Father. It doesn't really matter who or what helped me to believe this. What is important is the truth of my worth is found in Him; not in my performance of trying to measure up to an ever moving standard. I no longer felt like I was always first and ten, first and ten. I had scored a touchdown that night. Why, because I finally could accept the truth of my worth not in doing but in my being!

I have learned to reinforce this time and time again, over and over until now I truly know who I am. Remember, when you ask me how I am doing, I will say "I be's fine!" I believe I'm finally living in the truth that my worth is

> I believe I am finally living in the truth that my worth is not in what I do, but in whose I am.

not in what I do, but it is whose I am…the Great I can died to the glory of the Great I Am! You see, every disturbing situation, every deeply distorted belief, provides us with an opportunity to discover our incorrect thinking, to reject our worldly acquired beliefs and to exchange them for the truth. Robert McGee in his book, *The Search for Significance*, makes this point very strongly. I recommend his book for your pleasure. As an afterthought or rather a just occurred to me thought, I recommend Charles Solomon's book, *The Rejection Syndrome*. If you want to learn to challenge your "misbelieves", this book will be invaluable.

Let me close this section by using an illustration of the donkey in the dirt. A farmer had an old donkey he wanted to get rid of, so he dug a giant hole, put the donkey in it, and was simply going to fill the hole on top the donkey. The donkey had two choices, act or not act and die. He had to decide how to interpret the circumstances. The donkey looked at what was going on, and knew that he could either be covered up by the dirt or he could simply step on the new fresh dirt being piled in and eventually the farmer, would in fact, create his escape for him.

This is what I'm talking about. When I say, catching the critic, it is often that we are our own worst enemies (the critical self), and we make the wrong choices based on old learned imprinted beliefs. Rather than applying and acting on the truth that sets us free, we choose to stand still and act out of habit or patterned behavior! For the donkey, he choose to be set free by standing on the problem and not letting the problem stand on him! Cool! Let's take the next chapter to look at this concept of our being our own worst enemies a little closer.

To recap, this chapter offered ways or strategies to develop a proper perspective/attitude by:

--developing a Christian belief system

--constructing a realistic worldview reflecting your beliefs

--understanding a strategic awareness has great importance
--using spiritual tools

--stopping wrong thinking patterns

Quote: "What we think about when we are free to think about what we will—that is what we are or soon will become". A.W. Tozer

Chapter Five:
Do we like ourselves? Concepts
for a good self esteem!

"Love the Lord thy God with all your heart, and love thy neighbor as thy self"

Possibly the greatest hurdle I had to overcome was the hurdle of not believing in my self. God calls us to excellence, but our humanity calls us to comparison. Remember that we stated earlier that one unique aspect of man was that he was made to compare. Animals do not compare, a dog doesn't say I am an inferior dog; but he just goes on each day being his doggy self. When I was a doctoral student, I remember entering the class of eight students and always thinking, I was the least and didn't really belong in this group of potential scholars. I would never answer the questions for fear that I would be wrong and embarrass myself; often turning out to have the answer and then beating myself up for not answering. This then would lead to anger and frustration and an even deeper journey of the "poor poor me's". To conquer self image, to mold it to the biblical standard, achievable only in and by Christ, is paramount.

We are really in many ways our own worst enemies. How so? For one, we spend too much time inside our inner worlds, playing the blame or" who done it game". If we want to manage the ups and downs of life, and live up in a down world, you need to get up and get out, workout that which is within, avoid going down and in, move over and look up! The need to get up and get out is a statement of not staying inside your inner worlds all the time and to spend more time in your external world. The inner world can be like a cyclone, spinning tighter and tighter, until we spin out of control. We spin so fast as to finally loose perspective and to only be able to gaze at our negatives and see life as if in a dark and deep tunnel. What we need to do is get up and get out of our inward focus, stop circling thoughts with our own preoccupations and perceptions, seek help and clarification, and to get out in the world armed with a different perspective.

Life is for God's glory and when we center our focus on our own inner world, we live defeated because we are made to focus on Him. The very creation was made for the focus to be on the Maker, and not on man. As he is today, man focuses on himself, depression and anxiety goes up. Just look at the numbers of depression and anxiety cases we see in psychotherapy each day. This is not to say being depressed is a sin, but take the truth and examine for yourself if your focus is too much inward. It often helps me to get out and go to the mall or to a store and just watch people. I love to sit in the mall and watch people or go to the Big K and just read a book while in the presence of so many folks.

When I said get out, I hoped that you could see the "getting out" as getting out of your preoccupation with self analysis and get out to an "other focused" presentation. Be careful to understand, watching television or using other forms of "entertainment" , like video games or e-mail, is not other focused. The form of outward focus I hope will be to the benefit of others, a good application of your ministry gifts.

Let's restate a concept worth further investigation: If you want to avoid or manage the ups and downs of life, get up and get out, avoid being down and in, work out that which is within, and move over and look up! I have mentioned this in passing, but let us now take the time to examine this thought more carefully.

The idea of working out that which is within is the technique of becoming aware, working on the correction of those thoughts, and changing what your personality believes about itself. It is the examination of the "leftovers" of our childhoods. It is also the examination of how we can not take personal responsibility for the current situation we find ourselves in. Blame never solves, it only blames! The adversary so loves to keep us focused on our failures that we cannot live in the potentialities of our futures. The song I learned as a child teaches that I am a promise; I am a possibility, a great big bundle of potentiality! I am learning to make the right choice, and I am learning to hear God's voice. I am a great big promise of what God is going to make me to be! This might mean that I need to seek some help from others to help me to see how my past has affected my now. Therapy is not bad as along as the direction of the therapists is the direction of God being #1 in your priorities. God heals through the Holy Spirit, not techniques of psychology! God heals; after all, He is the Potter, we are the clay!

On top of this looking out, avoid going down and in is next. What I mean here is to avoid putting your head down. To avoid allowing yourself to live in the down side of remembering only the failures of your life, always notice where your head and eyes are focused and work to keep your thoughts such that your head is up. When it is down, where are your thoughts? It is true that our thoughts follow the direction of our eyes. The basic concept is that our mind is divided into quadrants and when we look with our eyes to certain directions or quadrants, our emotions follow. The quadrant of hope is up and out, not down and in. When you look down and in, you look to the emotions of failure and distress. Try it, it works; I guarantee! So try to live up and out and avoid down and in; except, in examining and processing growth through the Holy Spirit, as we acknowledge the trait and then giving it to the Spirit for correction and refinement.

To move over and look up is the spiritual part. For me, it means moving over into the obedience of the Word, actually stepping into the flow of the Holy Spirit, and then looking upward to find the strength and wisdom to proceed in a more likeable manner towards myself. The truth is, for us to ever life up, we need to learn to like ourselves and to claim the credentials of our heritage. Doubt self; doubt God and this is not a winning ticket. We say we do not have time for the priority of God; well if this be so, we will never like ourselves and we will never live in the victory or peace God promised. God must be a priority if we are to live up.

Just think about this for a second. How many times have you gotten or purchased a new toy and enjoyed it only to find in a brief time it is empty and boring and passé, a procured paid for emptiness good only for the credit card companies. E bay here I come! Later in the test we will talk of ways to move over and look up; for now, let us remember the priority of the upward focus and look to Him for life, not adult toys, like campers, recreation vehicles, and such!

A good personal devotional is a very credible way to start this moving over and looking up process. Just get started, do it out of a "required obedience". Do it intentionally. The promise in scripture is true. His word never returns void.

I want to warn us once again about the concept of codependency. My getting up and getting out does not give the power for my validation to others; it doesn't! What it does for me is provides the ability to find a different venue or a different place to check my thoughts. Codependency may be at the root of our not liking ourselves. Not owning our own worth is often a product of our childhoods, our histories or unresolved issues that create for us so much distortion. Let me give you an example from my own childhood.

I was in either preschool or kindergarten, while I lived in Monterey, California. I remember being called to the principal's office from what I used to call the box that God lived in. It was that brown wooden box that was just above the chalkboard. It was the intercom system, and when your name was called, the whole room looked at you, like life was coming to an end. I remember thinking that I must have done something dreadfully wrong. The box on the wall spoke, "Robert, come to the principals office".

I went into the hallway and met the hall monitor, who took me down to the principal's office. When I got inside, I looked over the counter and saw the secretary, God's best friend. I sat down in a chair, a chair that was too big for me and caused my feet to swing back and forth unable to touch the ground, how humiliating. Wanting to die, I waited for the inevitable. Soon the door opened to the principal's office and I thought I saw smoke coming out, a smoke indicating his eminence was ready to see me.

I walked inside, stood at full attention, and reported like a good little boy who had done something he just knew was wrong. The principal, Mr. Lightcap (funny how you remember things when you're scared) asked me to relax, but I couldn't -- I was the condemned! I was strong; I was ready for what ever the principal could do to me; after all, I was a bad little boy. I really believed this. Mr. Lightcap finally spoke and what he said rocked me back on my heels. He shared that I had been elected as the best behaved child in kindergarten and that I was going to receive a prize of a brand-new sleeping blanket and a beautiful goldfish, tank and all.

Wow! Why had I walked down the hall as the condemned criminal? So I have discovered that even in kindergarten, I was my own worst enemy. By the way, I remember my dad not wanting to take the goldfish on a trip from California to Georgia, so he flushed it down the commode and he told me that the fish was now in the ocean. I knew better, the fish was now in the septic tank. Good bye to my best and only prize!

Unless we own our own worth, overcome our pasts, begin to know ourselves, live in the awareness of the tiny bat syndrome, evaluate our own brokenness, realize our capacity for judgment, and give ourselves a chance to gain personal insights -- will always live down in a down world. It seems time now for us to look at how we can gain a sense of personal worth by taking a quick overview of ways to increase our self-esteem, how to access it, and how to grow in the image of Christ.

A. Thoughts and Definitions

"We only become what we truly are by the radical and deep seated refusal of that what others have made us to be" -- Jean Paul Sartre'. What a bold statement! Hugh Prather, in *Thoughts on Myself,* shares these

> *My security is not in what I think I am, but in whom You say I am.*

thoughts: "Often my desires are based on images of what I think I want to be. Perfectionism is slow death. Idols and ideals are based on the past. If everything were to turn out just as I would want it to, just as I would plan, I would never experience anything new. My life would be an endless repetition of stale successes. When I make a mistake, I experienced something unexpected. I sometimes react to mistakes as if I have betrayed myself. My fear of them seems to arise from the assumption that I'm potentially perfect and if I can just be very careful. I will not fall from heaven. But a mistake is a declaration of the way I am now, a jolt to the expectations I have unconsciously set, a reminder I am not dealing with the facts. When I have listened to my mistakes I have grown. And so has my self-concept."

One more quote by Maxwell Malty: "95% of all people in our society feel inferior about themselves." As an aside, the 5% may well contain several folks who falsely assume, by their own ego, a worth founded in achievement. This achievement is a sandy foundation, always subject to the world's eternal validation and worth. When we give others the ability to set our worth, we are always in danger of loosing the externalize value.

With these thoughts in mind, let's take a look at what self-esteem is, defined it, see what causes a low self esteem or concept, and then give a brief answer on what we can do to have a proper self-concept; which is necessary to living up in a down world. Let's go have some fun, shall we? Remember, we are not what we think we are, but rather we are what God has made us to be and that is the goal of a God reflected self-image. What we think we are so reflects the fallen sense of man.

Our self-image and our self-concept are somewhat synonymous. It is the picture we have of ourselves, as if a chief character in a book; the thoughts, attitudes, and feelings we have about ourselves. Self-esteem, on the other hand, means the evaluation an individual makes of his or her worth and significant. Self-image, in the end, is our self-description and self-esteem is our self-evaluation. What we want to look at in these paragraphs is our self-esteem. Remember that Christ saved a wretch like me. Would he have devoted so much time, if I were not worth it? The question becomes, can we overturn our poor self-concepts, our poor self-esteem, and begin to relate our worth through what the word of God says about us.

As an aside, here are just a few thoughts or "signposts" for us to contemplate. I have presented a strong case for the examination of our self esteem. The fear is always present that we easily self deceive; after all, the adversary is the "great deceiver". To anchor this fear, let's read a paragraph from Tozer, *The Incredible Christian*, page 109. "Almost all men live from childhood to death behind a semi opaque curtain, coming out briefly only when forced by some emotional shock and then retreating as quickly as possible into hiding again… only the man who knows he is sick (low self esteem) will go to a physician".

Lord, you said I can also say I am more than a conqueror. I can do all things in Christ, no matter what the circumstances are. My security is not in what I think I am, but in whom You say I am. I will arise and meet every day with joy and faiths, forgetting yesterday, save to learn the peace of your presence in it. I will become all that you have promised I can become. I am a child of the King, a servant of the God Most High, anointed, called and elected, and given the distinction of a meaningful purpose for this life. There is where I find my self-esteem. I will arise each day and go to the Father. Thank you Lord!

What is self esteem? Self-esteem is a state of feeling fine about who you are, a deep down in your soul feeling. It is the experience of feeling that you're worthy of happiness and capable of managing life's challenges. It is a feel-good combination of self-confidence and self-respect. It's having the gumption to ask for a job promotion or raise, and it's the inner grit that keeps you going, no matter what the answer. Self-esteem isn't everything, it's just that there's nothing without it. Of course we know that the nothing can only be supplied by the words of the Spirit. Self-esteem is also the courage to act, even if you may fail; even if you may humiliate yourself all over again. Knowing what self-esteem is and defining it is essential.

It might also be helpful if we knew what good high self-esteem looked like, what are some of the signs of high self-esteem. Typically someone who has high self esteem also has a sense of security. They can ask the question "what will become of me?" They have a sense of belonging. This is one of the essential needs of today. We live in a culture so isolated that we often do not belong in or to anything. We may go to things, events, support groups; but we need to find a sense of belonging to proffer peace and high esteem. It is also a sense of finding purpose in life. This may in fact be one of the most difficult concepts of self-esteem, finding your purpose.

Briefly, and I mean briefly, the answer for developing self esteem comes in the close walk with the presence of the Spirit. I wished I had the time to talk about the will of God, but I will say at this point, that there is no singular purpose that God has made us for. I really don't believe that there's just one single purpose, but that rather God has a flow for our lives and we need to stay close to him. By using the concepts of upward living we might hear His purposeful will for our lives. I pray that you're finding your purpose, and I pray that this book might help.

I can take the time to say these few brief thoughts about the will of God. I believe that we need to ask three very basic questions about seeking the will of God for our lives. Do other people tell us we are good at something, that it seems our gift? Do we enjoy what it is others affirm us in? Lastly, is there anything in the Word of God to prohibit us from doing this action or will? Balance these thoughts with the understanding that God is providential in our lives and go for the joy of the journey! A great exposition of the will of God is offered by Leslie Weatherhead in his book, *The Will of God*. Let's return to defining the concept of self esteem.

A high self-esteem is characterized by a personal competence and pride; this being the ability to feel confident to meet the challenges of life. This sense of personal power comes from the empowerment of the Holy Spirit. It grows more and more in our "being", as we process successes and carefully remember that God was the author and finisher of each one of our own personal success stories. This is critical. What I am saying here is that we often give credit to ourselves, and this sets up a false sense of security because in ourselves we can do nothing. You may think this silly, but it is critical that we understand that we are nothing except what we are made by God in Christ to be.

It tells us in the book of Ephesians, chapter 2, versus eight through 10; "For it is by grace you have been saved, through faith, and this not from yourselves, it is the gift of God -- not by works, so that no man can boast. For we are God's workmanship, created in Christ Jesus to do good works, which God prepared in advance for us to do". (NIV) What this is telling us is that when we understand who we really are, we understand that everything we do comes out of who He is, and this always to His glory. This is subtle; but disregarded, it leads to ego and pride in self! Ask the Father to anchor this truth in your mind.

High self-esteem also demonstrates that the person has a deep sense of trust. This means believing in something outside of ourselves; and of course, this for me means believing and trusting that God is sufficient. To doubt self is actually to doubt God and to call him insufficient for our needs; and in turn, insufficient to meet His purposes for His world. Trust is not something that we have to have earned, or something we require others to do for us to trust; but rather it is an attribute of faith that we give. I will, and I determine to live my life, trusting God, and that He is sufficient for my life. You might imagine that this takes regular examination of your thoughts. This is where I practice the concept of 3 x 5 cards, where I put the word trust in my environment to remind me to trust God. It's a good technique, and you might imagine that I have many 3 x 5 cards; one of them being to access peace in my life…all the time, everyday day

I am going to list the following signs of high self-esteem in a somewhat rapid succession. I do not want to over emphasize the idea of knowing what it looks like, but I did want us to have some sense of what we're achieving our striving for. A sense of responsibility, a sense of contribution, a sense of making real choices and decisions, a sense of self-discipline and self-control, and a sense of encouragement are all attributes of a high self-esteem or high self-concept. Essential, at least in this author's thinking, is that high self-esteem reflects an environment of encouragement, support, and a strong sense of belonging to a healthy family.

This is the role that the corporate church plays in today's culture. I believe that the reason that many of us suffer from low self-concept is that we are a people who are so isolated. In this isolation, we validate ourselves on our own poor self images, without the valuable validation of an encouraging outsider.. We listen to our own old tapes and do not get the affirmation and reflection of the body of Christ that we find in a family called the church. Unless our culture somehow returns to the priority or need for community, there is going to be a need for even more therapists and more medications… this I believe!

Let's move on and look at the why's of low self-esteem. To reflect an old song, maybe not so old for some of you, "What's it all about Alfie?" This song was popular not so many years ago and meant a lot to me. The why's of low self esteem are not that complicated, so let's proceed.

B. The Why's and Causes of Low Self Esteem

Very often the primary cause of low self-concept is our own thinking. We are creatures of choice, and often we make the choice to literally stay down. In a very subconscious way, we keep our sense of worth buried, so that the expectations people have on us will not increase and so that in some way we can receive a secondary gain, or to put it another way, we can receive attention or pity. In the book, *Happiness is A Choice*, Drs. Minirth and Meier make the strong point that for many the choice to not get better, or to keep a low self-concept, has very direct and positive side benefits, well worth more than the necessary choice to change. By not making a willful decision to change our "learned histories", we keep our chosen low self-concept from increasing.

How exactly important is a healthy, realistic, reflected self concept or self esteem? Monumental! The fact that we would filter all our thinking through a "deceived belief", about oneself, flavors everything we do. It is solely the most damaging affecter of our very being, founded in the Father. To be up we must take a determined, willful examination of self.

This being true, the fear is that most of us will not take the journey of self discovery, fearing what we might find. We fear an adjustment in attitude that could be deflating; or at the other end of the pendulum, inflating enough to cause us to become response-able to the Spirit; and thus, called to action. Upward living is purposeful and meaningful leading to a productive well defines life.

This pursuit of a biblically based self image is so critically important to us in the pursuit of living up with God. We would do well to immediately do whatever it takes to remove the disguise and permit our real selves to be known. To be known, certainly for the Kingdom, and also known by yourself. Romans 12:3 tells us to take a sober estimation of ourselves; sober as to honest, genuine, and real.

In somewhat the same way, we determine how others see us. If we feel badly about ourselves, we project an image of someone who does not have it together. For example; if I feel fat, I will wear non complimentary clothing. I wear clothing that does not tuck in, often black, and I project the image that I feel like I'm overweight. I don't project self-confidence, because it is true that I choose how others see me. If I see myself as Christ does, then the projection is quite different. It is more confidant and self-assured when seen through the eyes of a redeemed image. By the way, this idea of weight is so much an imposed American view of weight and what is acceptable, or so I feel.

Our self-concepts have often been "predetermined" for us, showing up as these distortions of our own histories. We have the baggage of our childhoods, our old learned behaviors, the perspectives we have taken on life, our attitudes; and of course, our ever present cognitive "stinking thinking" that pervades our personality. We're often feeling pressured to think poorly of ourselves. It is not always all right for the Christian to have a good self-concept.

In some circles or religious cultures, this "good image" is seen as sin. Let me offer this explanation. We live in a world of relativity, a world of "I ism". Our fear of the future, our guilt of the past, our "fishbowls" and world expectations, all cause for us the lessening of self worth or value. We have a need to please; and if we are going to please, we had better be careful not to outshine too many people. Humbleness is next to godliness, right? Yes, but here no! This is classic self-righteousness. I hope that we will be careful to examine what it means when someone tells us to be careful of being too prideful. To say, "I have done this" is not to deny that in the doing of this that God was not critically involved. God can be assumed as being the author and finisher of all that the Christian does. I know the plans I have made for you (Jeremiah 29:11).

So the question becomes, "Do I choose to get to know and love myself?" I'm afraid that often, because of a lot of reasons, the answer is no. If this is true for you, acknowledge it, own it, and ask the Holy Spirit to help you to change. It seems like I always come back to this, but I believe it to be the simplest and most direct way to live up in a down world.

We just are not people who live very self-aware and when we acknowledge our areas of growth, not weaknesses, we give the Holy Spirit a chance to make the impact that God wants in and for our lives.

Parenthetically, I do not believe that we have within our personality areas of weakness; but rather, that we have areas of growth. Areas of growth are parts of our personality that others have stated we need to improve or seek spiritual growth in. This insight then turns these areas of growth into strengths. Again I say, God did not make junk. It is our perception of what God made that makes it seem like junk...not junk, just junky thinkers...us! In 1Timothy 4:4-6 these thoughts are shared: "for everything God created is good and nothing is to be rejected if it is received with thanksgiving, because it is consecrated by the Word of God and prayer. If you point these things out to the brothers, you will be a good minister of Jesus Christ, brought up in the truths of the faith and of the good teachings that you have followed". (NIV) You see it's all gravy baby, no problems! Thanks Steve!

Unfortunately one of the largest causes of low self-concept is the history of inadequate parent-child relationships. Very often, children are raised up in a critical, shame-based system. In this family system, the children are taught rejection, they're scolded often, and they're made to feel less than adequate; often due to the parents own inadequacies. Parents set unrealistic goals and expectations, they

> *We dislike ourselves in direct proportion to the amount of rejection and criticism we experience in childhood.*

inadvertently teach their children to expect failure, they rarely give praise or encouragement and compliments are never heard. The children are punished repeatedly and harshly, cuddling or touching is avoided, and these frightened parents often overprotective or dominate their children.

The shame based child grows up always trying to achieve, in reality often being very successful; nonetheless, never quite being enough no matter what accolades are poured on. This sets up a value in doing, not an intrinsic value in being just an "exceptional child" of God.

There are three very common unrealistic expectations that are enemies of our self-acceptance. *I must meet other people's standards*, if I am to be loved. Whenever I failed to reach my goals or expectations I need to be pressured, shamed, frightened or punished. *I must seek to master my world*, to be in charge, to be smart, to be the center of my environment, and to make my own decisions. This is the perfect setup for a Type A, driven, highly intense personality. The deep injury is this; *the person drives himself or herself to feel good only in an effort to cover up a low self-concept* they don't even understand. We call this the setting up of a double bind system, where the child never knows whether he or she is up or down, loved or cursed, cherished or just a bother or burden.

C. What can we do?

Access and expect peace, know contentment, realize the worth of self as you find your divinely appointed meaning and purpose. Live in the now and let go of the guilt and fears of the past. Look to the future with hope. *Remember, we are what we were taught, we are what we believe, we are a collection of believed perceptions, and we are who we believe we think we are.* So think of yourself through the mind of Christ!

I want to approach this section in two ways. First I want to list eight concepts that build self-esteem and then lastly I would like to share a formula I developed using three steps of recovery. Let's look first at these concepts that build self-esteem. The concepts that build self-esteem are: accept yourself right now; look inside yourself, not outside; stop judging yourself and others, be a "good finder" and "intend to extend"; separate the you from your behavior; avoid comparing and competing; know that you are doing your best; practice unconditional loving, focused ability; and, stop blaming others and start taking responsibility for your own life.

Does this sound like what the world is teaching today? Not really! I believe these concepts are somewhat self-explanatory, and hope that you will pause long enough to take each one into careful consideration. For now, however, let's move on to the three steps of recovery.

Step 1: Assessment

We need to do some housekeeping! What does doing some housekeeping mean? All of us come with baggage. All of us come with some old tapes that need to be changed. It doesn't matter whether we came from a really healthy family or whether we came from a dysfunctional family; everyone needs to do some housekeeping. This involves assessing what goes into your self-concept. You might want to call this redecorating the house.

You ask yourself these types or kinds of questions: what are the beliefs I carried from my childhood that affect how I think and feel about myself; what memories do I have that still hurt and cause pain and how does that affect the way I present myself; did I come out of adolescence feeling valued, unique, or gifted and special; how do I handle rejection and what from my old tapes is causing the disruption; and, you might also ask yourself or others what is their perceived sense of your self worth and what can you discover that came out of "believed perceptions" of your youth. What is your physical image of yourself? Positive or always trying to be something or someone physically you just aren't. Are you self-conscious, does it matter a great deal to you about what others think and are you always seeming to be a "people pleaser" or never making waves? Is your motto in life, peace at all cost? It would be helpful to ask yourself; do I want my way, do I want the have fun all the time, and do I want to be in control? Or do I want to be left alone and sit quietly on the sidelines. Each of these positions describes a different way of looking at your self worth, each has value in the arrived at answer.

Do we need to look at our expectations in life? Are they low, too high, unrealistic, undetermined, confusing, nondescript, or just plain impossible? If you can't discern this for yourself, often a good friend can help with your goals and expectations if you will give the time and energy to listen. I am asking you to listen and not reflect their thoughts with your counterattacks. Be careful about the need to always win and learn to listen and reflect back to the speaker what he or she is saying. Repeat what they said if you feel it necessary to make sure you heard their thoughts and not just your defenses!

Take a look at your hopes and your dreams. How do they seem to match up with your spiritual gifting? Are you filled up in life, is your life about passion and are you living with intensity, integrity, and "intentionality"? All of these are ways to asses the strength of your self worth. Do you allow people to impose on you work and do you seem to be unable to say no to anyone? Take a look at what it is you are doing and if it is not a passion and something that you look forward to, and literally wake up excited to do, examine why are you doing it…pressure from work, parental messages of worth, or a "driven" nature to achieve and climb the ladder. This is the process of assessment and these questions are just a few of the thoughts needed here.

At this juncture, I would hope and request that you take the time to reflect on these markers for self assessment. It is vital that we ask these questions, dialogue about them, use a good friend, and discover the "roots of our worth". This reflective nature is so foreign to the culture of today. S.T.O.P.; get still, think, organize your thoughts, and proceed with peace. Please STOP! Remember, the goal is a humility founded through Christ, a believed and acknowledged true sense of worth used to His glory…soli Gloria deo.

It has been said by Dr. Larry Crabbe, Dr. James Dobson, and others; a sense of security is vital for the work of the personality. I can't imagine trying to live up without a sense of the security we have in love of God. This security, certain and eternal, expressed in the great commandment to love God and to love yourself. The lack of God confidence, expressed in self concept/confidence, is a security in self so needed to achieve the peace promised. So, please, examine and practice self awareness. You can do all things through Christ (Ph 4:13).

Lastly, what are the alternative thoughts I can develop to help me with the concerns that the above questions raised? I literally identified over fifty statements I was making about myself and from these statements I gained the insights needed to overcome my life imposed artificial mask I was wearing. The basis of all of my "axiomatic thoughts" or believed perceptions was that I had to make peace at all costs and that my role in the family was to settle the issues and to be the "clown" to break the tension. Now, this tension may or may not have been actual. The point is that from my perception it was. Not guilt on my family here, this is my "little red wagon" and I am the driver of this ship. Peace!

So for me, the teachings of challenging my thinking and looking at the drawn conclusions became very important. Assessment is something you can do yourself and you do not necessarily need instruments or help; but I want to make it clear that often we are unable to look at ourselves clearly and taking a spiritual inventory or taking a personality inventory is helpful and certainly not something the scripture would prohibit. You can access any number of instruments on the web by simply typing in psychometrics and defining the search to personality or self-concept measurements. So what is step two?

Step 2: Strengthen your position

Personal acceptance is critical. You might ask why and the answer is that if you cannot accept who you are, you cannot change. The ability to nurture s good self accept is the basis for the needed changes. To not accept oneself for who you are is the concept called denial, or if more serious, it could be delusional thinking. If you fear that you are having trouble here, seek some help from your pastor or a good friend to determine what the emotional blockage is. Remember; never replace your self-concept until you have another belief to stand in that works. What I am sharing is to never replace a coping mechanism without first supplying a back up system to rely on. This adequate back-up replacement is assurance of grace!

Accept who you are and know that change is coming and it is going to be a great journey. A short story might help here. I remember the story of a rabbit that was always complaining of the fact that his ears hung down and all the other rabbit's ears stood straight up. So, one day, in deep despair, he climbed up in a tree and hung upside down for a long, long time. He began to feel accepted because finally his ears went straight out from his head. A wise owl came by and questioned the rabbit about his precarious position. The rabbit answered that he was not happy with himself and wanted to be just like all the other rabbits, so there he hung…upside down and looking swell just like the other rabbits. The owl sighed and shook his head. "Silly rabbit' he said. "Don't you know you are special and precious? Don't you know that you are unique and singularly made by God? Oh rabbit, you are a lope eared rabbit, a one of a kind super creation." With that revelation, the rabbit hopped off in the realization that he was after all, quite special.

We are not so unlike this rabbit in the story. How often do we compare ourselves to others and never seem to measure up? So we allow the Spirit to bolster our self-concept and we listen to others as they reflect the wonder that they see. Be open to compliments. We often aren't, we do not accept compliments well. We often discount them or deny they are true. Move actively to accomplish and realize the things that you can change or don't like about you and accept the things you can't and stop worrying about those, and let go and let God. This is like the Serenity Prayer of AA. Cause it to "fit "now. Let who you are bloom now, inadequate or not, bloom! If the birds that can sing well only sang, then none of us learning to sing would ever make a noise. Use what you have now, and seek the growth God has in mind.

As you grow, learn to lean to your self more and lean in to others less. This might seem a contradiction, but what is meant here is to look carefully at how much you rely on others for your sense of purpose and value. It does not mean to isolate, but to assess and strengthen your own "water legs" and let go of others pontoons and stop using others as a primary life raft. Be self-affirming. Your redeemed spirit is able. Tell yourself the truth when you have succeeded. Call yourself a winner. Go ahead; be self-congratulatory.

This following thought is one of my favorite ways to strengthen our self worth. Get involved in your passionate ministry. If you are a Christian operating without an expression of your gifts being used for others; you are like the sponge that never gets wrung out, it dries out and cracks and crumbles. Each of us has a gift. I Corinthians 12:7 makes it clear, "Now to each one

> *Know thyself, accept thyself, and esteem thyself!*

the manifestations of the Spirit are given for the common good". (NIV) Know your gift and do your ministry. You will atrophy sitting on the sidelines.

Our churches do not need any more pew sitters, we are no longer able to be the YMCA where members pay dues and the staff caters to their membership needs. We must be a people going out and taking the YMCA to the neighborhood. Your gifts are needed, every single one of them. To be a member of the body and not use your body gifts in ministry is an oxymoron. Self-esteem will increase as your devotion to the use of your gifts goes up. The Spirit will affirm you and you will feel passion and energy like never before. Trust me, try it. What's more, specialize at something and get real good at the one thing you do well.

Little David was sitting under the tree playing his one string while he was watching the sheep. Along came this judger of others, this "nay sayer" who told little David he was just using one string. He wasn't hip like the other dudes with 12 strings. Little David looked up at the man and shook his head. He may have only one string but he knew he was good on that one string. Don't let others be your judge. You be the judge. Avoid blaming behaviors, this only feeds the defense mechanisms we develop to feel safe; and safe doesn't grow anything but more hurt. Plato once implied: Know thyself, accept thyself, and esteem thyself!

Your self concept is strongly predicated on what others have said about us. The ability to strengthen your position has most to so with challenging the negative self talk, paying close attention to what you say about yourself, learning to "register and acknowledge" self statements is a sure fire way to create a biblical, scriptural sense of worth.

Step 3: Accept and Stabilize

Accept the peace of God, know the contentment of the Spirit, and realize the worth of self as you find your meaning and purpose. An awareness of self-purpose is one of the things that set us apart from the animals. We can define who we are and then attach a value to it. Of course, as we have already stated, the

> *Be aware of the critic, that side of you that is always self-depreciating. Talk back to Him.*

problem is we humans compare and judge. To avoid this judgment from others, we set up defenses or barriers to being truly known. They include blame hurling, getting anger, being a perfectionist, bragging, lying and stretching the truth, making excuses all the time, and other self medication issues; such, as alcohol, overeating, drugs, or being workaholic.

Finally, "catch the critic". I alluded to this earlier, but here is where it really fits and makes its strongest application. Be aware of the critic, that side of you that is always self depreciating. Talk back to him. Use a howitzer style mantra to counter the attack. What I mean by this, is come back with a furious counter attack of self appreciations and affirmations. Say stop it to yourself and learn to catch the "tiny bat" that you have taken out of your pocket once again. Ask, what does the critic cost me? It costs me everything. The critic says, "There is no intrinsic value in a life, only a potential for doing something worthwhile". Do you see the deep danger here? This is an emphasis on what you do and not on who you are!

The value that the critic finds is not in the person, but in the act. This is so wrong and so pervades our culture today. Look at the value we put on sports and on the athletics programs of our schools. Wrong! Our real self is found not in what we do but in the ultimate realization and revelation of our value being found in whose we are and for whom we do it. It is our being, not our doing. We can never do enough, because their will always be someone to say we are not doing enough. The critic has been taught to value performance, not heritage. Remember, this horrible critic is you! Catch your own thoughts and bring them under the cross! Please learn unconditional grace and the freedom of the work of Christ finished and realized in each of us! Right thinking plus directed behaviors equal solid self-esteem! For more insights into self-esteem I recommend the books: *Self esteem*, by Matthew M. Key and *Who do you think you are?* by Joel Wells.

Remember, my favorite key to strengthen self concept is to get involved in the live of others through your own God given ministry. Luke 9:23, "If any man will come after me, let him deny himself, take up his cross daily, and follow me". I believe the cross is our ministry. John 15:13, "Greater love hath no man than this, but that he lay down his life for a friend". This life being laid down is ministry, the serving of others, being "other focused" and seeking to minister. Seek ministry now! Remember to give yourself away.

Zig Zigler, past president of the Southern Baptist Convention, and popular motivational speaker, reminds us that you can get anything in life you want if we will help enough other people get what they want. Ken Blanchard, football star, tells us you can help others maximize their potential by catching them doing things right. This is so true for children. You see, it's not so important who you are, but rather what you do with the "who they are" that counts. Give your self away, do it in the power of the Spirit; and then, stress will also not be a problem. How often do we say things like "give it to God" or "do it in the Spirit". Is this a major saying or is this really something to be done or is it actually doable. It is not so much doable as it is speaking and believable. We don't do letting go, we speak and believe it as part of our spirits, and then the Spirit acts with our submission and does in us what we cannot do by steps, or procedures, or 1,2,3's. See what I mean? *It is not something you do; it is someone you become by the conscious application of bathing your mind in the things of*

God, finding your priorities, properly focusing and in practicing being around the works and factions of the Kingdom.

What are these practices and factions of the Kingdom? Speak the truth from the heart, never fib or make something up; seek to minister and find the good in all and all situations; walk your talk and live in high integrity, live intentionally and intensely; do it now, do it first, don't wait for a kindness to act; don't wait for the return kindness to feel good or appreciated; and, love God while he uses you to meet the hopes and needs of others. Be "other focused", sincere, and willing to go the extra mile while you seek the rest and peace for the energy needed to be about your calling. Broker T. Washington sums it up in this statement: "There are two ways of exerting one's strength; one is pushing down, the other is pulling up."

Once again, I want to strongly recommend the book, *Making a Life with God*, by Dan Wolpert. The cornerstone of the power is in our relationship to and with God. We need to recognize our centeredness in Him, practice spiritual disciplines, and abide if we are to have the strength and the ability to do any ministry at all. A ministry founded in your own energies and dreams, dies a shorten life and soon death! We call it burnout when really it is burn up, burning up in our own power.

What is needed to prevent burn up is to let God in! Let Him in by surrendering your unmet needs to God; allow God to serve you in ways only He can; trust God to grow your self esteem; work on fulfilling and building your own renewed worth by strong self affirmation; listen to your self, trust your gut instincts; remind yourself constantly that God builds winners; and, be certain of this, you belong to God! He made you for Him.

Chapter Six:
Stress Management Skills and Overview

Stress is a comprehensive and very sophisticated field of study. I wish to make it clear that in no way will I attempt to cover the field of research available in the many and massive texts. There are entire texts devoted to nothing but stress, and often these texts deal with only one aspect of stress. Venture it to say, what I will present in the following chapter are my unique thoughts, which match up with the overall concept of making life work and living up; and, I will look at the parallel between living in the now and the stress it creates when we don't. I will go further and try to express a few techniques that work for me in the effort to reduce or live with stress.

Our stress is self-created, in large degree, by the ways we divert from the mind and thinking of the scripture. I entirely agree with Dr. Lloyd Ogilvie in his book, *Making Stress Work for You*, when he says, "Our reactions to people follow the same pattern. Until

> *In my words, stress management is best practiced when we adopt a focus on life by living in the now and then practice bringing all our thoughts and situations to the obedience of the scripture.*

our thinking is conditioned with God's love and acceptance, we will physiologically react to the stress of competition, hostility, or impatience. The key to managing stress is allowing the Lord to indwell, condition, and control what happens in the cortex and in the sub cortical structures of our brain. When we allow God to abide in us, the reasoning portion of our brain can be brought into unity with our physiologic systems. The secret of managing stress is bringing our thoughts, emotion and physical response under the control of the mind of Christ." (Page 12)

In my words, stress management is best practiced when we adopt a focus on life by living in the now and then practice bringing all our thoughts and situations to the obedience of the scripture. This takes time, conscientious application of concepts for guarding our minds, and the use of simple, "memorable techniques of being still with Him". Why you might ask? To live longer, more peacefully, less anxious, and to be an example for the world; to be salty, that is the reason.

Can the Christian be stressed? Yes, but living to our best is an example to others. I want to take the time now and give a very general overview of my thoughts on stress. Later in the chapter I will further define and expand these basic premises.

A. Basic thoughts

Congratulations, you've been promoted. It's fun to picture how you'll spend the extra money. But along with the new rewards may come a sudden increase in your duties at work. You might feel stressed by having to shoulder these added responsibilities; especially if you have to adapt other changes to your life at the same time. That stressed feeling may actually help you cope. It can pump you up to work extra hard to get organized and figure out how to do more in the same amount of time. So your promotion illustrates the rule that not all stress is bad; it's all in how you handle it. This type of stress is often referred to as "U stress". It is helpful if properly managed. Remember, stress in only managed, never avoided; manageable not avoidable.

Professor Hans Seyle spent much time studying the effect of mental responses on the body, and he has defined stress as "the response of the organism to the demands which are placed upon it". In other words, the stress itself is not exactly the problem, but is how we handled it or fail to handle it that matters. We often add to the stress by wrong ways of dealing with it. We may try to dismiss our troubles or set to the side instead of taking care of them. Stress is a universal thing today, and there are over 30 million people with high blood pressure in this country. When Dr. Lloyd Ogilvie, conducted a recent survey, he discovered that people believe that the largest problem we're facing today is stress. We have many heart and blood pressure disturbances, which could be eliminated if we would take better care of the stressed in our lives. Millions of people have ulcers, irritable bowel syndrome, colitis and other digestive system disturbances due to stress.

What happens when you feel stressed out? Most people feel they need to cut some corners. Adequate sleep and exercise are usually among the first things to go. No harm done, right? Not so. Activity and rest are nature's prime stress relievers, and skipping or skimping on them will just compound your problems. On the job, you work less efficiently, taking longer to do each test, falling further behind, and feeling even more like a victim of stress. Deprived of exercise and sleep, you're likely to become more irritable, flying off the handle easier.

Recent studies have shown that anger can trigger a cascade of stress hormones, and chronic anger may eventually raise the risk of life-threatening illness. Stress can worsen high blood pressure, ulcers, stomachaches, headaches and back pain. So, what to do? Earn big dividends by working conscientiously at these ideas. Keep in mind that enjoyment, happiness, harmony, and joy are all mental responses, which help reduce tension and stress.

Next time you find yourself under pressure, going in a few days or weeks with little sleep and virtually no exercise, think twice. Sure, it's not easy to find the time to get enough sleep and exercise, particularly during a busy stretch. But you'll find that by taking that time, it will pay off big dividends. Get enough sleep, whatever it takes to make you feel thoroughly rested the next morning, for some people, it's nine hours, and for others it might be six. A good rule of thumb is to select a time, let's say eight hours, and then set your alarm clock 15 minutes earlier. If you wake up feeling rested, then eight hours is what you need. If you wake up tired on a consistent basis, then go to nine hours and repeat the process. This will help you find what your body needs for adequate rest. Work out regularly and get the exercise that your body needs. Do an activity you really enjoy doing. Exercise helps take the lid off the pressure building up inside of you. The best advice I seem to be able to garnish from all that's being written today is to try to exercise at least 20 minutes, vigorously three times a week. This really isn't too much to ask for the big dividends it will pay.

Do one thing at a time, breaking big projects into small chores. Stay focused on the task at hand. Watch out for what I call "polyphasic behavior", where we jump from task to task and try to manage too many things at one time.

For me it is often helpful to use a checklist and to work on one item a time, systematically checking each item off as it occurs. It's also helpful for me to close my study door and try to find a concentrated time, hopefully without too many distractions.

Give yourself a chance to calm down, but taking time out for complete rest and relaxation. This can be as simple as a 20-minute rest and relaxation session each day. I use the concept of accessing peace, where I spend some time meditating and find myself imagining that I am in a quiet and calm place. I systematically relax my body and give myself a chance to think only of my being in this valley or peaceful scene.

Say "No" to and set limits on undue claims for your free time. This is not easy and is in fact one of my most difficult areas to overcome. My secretary has tried everything including putting up a sign in the office saying, "No is a word too!" Thanks Virginia, keep up the good work. It might help to examine the reasons that you feel you need to be so available. For many pastors, and well caring Christians, it is probably about the need to be needed. This again goes back to the concept of codependency; a wanting to fill emptiness by doing for others rather than healing the wounds of rejection that live inside due to past hurts and misunderstandings. I recommend the reading of *Healing the Inner Child*, by Dr, Charles Whittaker, if this seems a big stressor for you. I list books to help you know that it is not my intention to be exhaustive, but informative and a roadmap to living up!

Share your feelings with family, friends and co-workers, or if need be, a counselor. Your pastor has been trained in good listening skills and the effort of just getting feelings off your chest, or the pure catharsis often is enough. This is not easy for many of us from the northern European region. I remember sharing a sermon one Sunday and before I started the service, I went out into the congregation to say hello. I had not lived long in North Dakota and did not know the privacy concerns of the local farmer. I reach out to shake a man's hand and he just didn't want to. I moved on. After the service, he walked up to me and shared a good hearty welcome, but only after he knew who I was. This is not bad, but illustrates how difficult this can be for some of us, healthful nonetheless.

Keep your sense of humor. I will speak extensively in the coming pages about this, but suffice it for now to say, laughter puts stress in perspective. Laughter also helps rally the body's defenses against pain and disease. Laughter is the number two best release for stress. Did you hear the one about…? It is curious for me that we do not understand the need for laughter. Keep in mind 5 year olds laugh four hundred times more each day than we do as adults…Huh!

Learn to choose and access peace. I spoke of this in an earlier chapter and it is critical. At all times, attempt to have an attitude of ministry and peace to others, this will help. Finally, as an overview, learn to live in the now. This will be the subject of much of the next few pages. The future belongs to worry and the past belongs to guilt—not true. God says he supplies all of our needs according to his riches in glory and this tells us that nothing is going to happen to us today that God did have in the big scope and that there is nothing He can't handle. There are really no coincidences, just opportunities for God to work in the happenings of our lives. He is always there.

B. Basic, Very Basic Stress Management Skills found in Scripture

Effectiveness in life is not in the thought to do but in the application of doing. Be ye doers of the word, and not hearers only. Faith is completed or perfected by doing works of God for Him through him. We are to act upon the works of God (Matthew 7:24, NIV). As we put our hands to work for the diligent are made rich (Proverbs 10:46). The point is to do, not just read. We must be prepared for the life circumstances that create stress; it is often the case however, that we are not reacting to

> *Effectiveness in life is not in the thought to do but in the application of doing.*

stress in a very non-proactive preventive way. We are caught off guard and "penniless" as to what to do. No money in the bank, no reserves of practiced behavior in the reservoir. Let's attempt a definition of stress as a precursor to sharing some of the skills from the scripture, and this briefly.

Stress is the pressure of life on the organism of human existence and personality! As life happens, stuff, thoughts and feelings come into the psychic membrane seen here as the parabolic sphere. As these thoughts come in, we are trained to process them and then discharge them into the outer spaces of our non-present realities. When we don't discharge these thoughts they build up, stay trapped in our emotions, and eventually form their own protective walls (defenses) and they become "encapsulated danglings". After a period of time, these "danglings" build up to the point that we must explode or implode. To explode is the common means of stress relieve in the male and to implode is the common stress reliever for the female.

It is true that due to the wiring of the brain hemispheres, and the fact that women have more connective tissue between the hemispheres, that they process life much more completely. They suffer from depressive related stress reactions much more than men. Men tend to just get angry and run off to forget it even happened in a short time. No bias here, just the facts!

I want to make a strong point here. Dr. Archibald Hart shares in his book *Male Depression*, suggests that the male is a great deal more likely to depression than is commonly thought. If stress is a major factor in your life, male or female, investigate a low grade depression. This cause of stress is often misdiagnosed or totally untreated.

Eventually, what occurs is the loss of equilibrium or we have equilibrium imbalance and we drop below the homeostatic safety line. This places us in great danger of emotional issues; to include depression, aggressive behaviors, and even suicide. What we need to do is go back into the psychic and retrieve

> *Stress is any occasion, which we perceive to be inconsistent with the way we think it should be, whether major or minor.*

these danglings, process them through the truth and wisdom of God's word, examine them and create a new way of dealing with the emotions, and this in turn releases them to be processed and they no longer are an internal pressure. . This process was shared in the section on right thinking. Once we empty out the membrane, our conscious and subconscious memories, the pressure decreases and the mind returns to equilibrium and homeostatic balance is returned.

This is part of the reason I think the Bible teaches us to never go to bed with unresolved anger or issues that have not been given to prayer and needful forgiveness. We hold on and the result is built up resentments that create this imbalance. It is amazing when we realize just how well God has really equipped us for stress if we would only use his principles for life. Stress is not really about the physical; it may after all be all about the spiritual. *It is about loneliness for God.*

What I am referring to here is not staying close enough to God in our determined practices of discipleship. This does not imply performance, but rather, the "new Man" doing the things that substantiate the "new man" within us all. Stress is created as we distance ourselves from the source of tranquility. Actually, for God stress can be good, as we know that we grow in tribulation, and this growth produces peace in the long run! Aren't we in this for the long run? I think so!

Honesty is critical. Do we have a substantial investment with our spiritual development? Do we consider first the answers or solutions found in Christ first? It is such a natural, trained cultural phenomenon to not consider stress and Christ as connected. Please develop your faith ...Facing **All I t**rust **Him.**

Stress is any occasion, which we perceive to be inconsistent with the way we think it should be, whether major or minor. Stress is the reaction of the personality to change. We don't like change. How many Presbyterians did it take to change a light bulb? The answer: Four commissions and two committees and a vote of the Session. Remember, move the piano one-inch at a time! How many Lutherans? None! Change, what is that?

We cannot eliminate stress from our lives. We can only manage its effects by what we do and by the way we think about the stressor. Stress is not good or bad, it just is. There is good stress and bad stress, "U-stress or D-stress". We are servants of God, but still stress confronts us. Paul was always careful to move his life through the knowledge of Christ, and His ever presence. The Christian does not have to give into troubles, because when rightfully thinking, we know that we are not alone and that the power of God is operating in our good favor. Lest this sound like pie in the sky, remember, that most of what we do is actively place our hearts and minds in the position and the Lord does the work of peace production. Everyone gets both sun and rain as it tells us in Matthew 5:45b. Jesus said we would have tribulations, but be of good cheer; we shall also have peace in knowing He has overcome the world. Do you truly believe this? How do you apply in your daily lives? Stress is a tool that the Adversary will use to discourage us. He uses it to adversely affect our growth in Christ. Remember, the daily application of cleansing prayer and confronting the stressors as they occur.

Once again, we cannot control the stressors of life that come in on us, they just are. They are not right or wrong. The feelings and the thinking come in freely. Stressors timing may not be controlled, but we can control our thinking and our doing by carefully and consistently applying practices of right thinking combined with right actions or doings. Stress results when we adopt a worldview contrary to God's expressed view in the Word. *Remember, that the right perspective of grace, as stated earlier, is critical.* When we see ourselves as new creatures, condemnation and guilt are not available to the mind for stress producing confusion.

Take each day as it comes...live in the now! When we live in the now it means that we have relegated the past to forgiveness and repentance and the future to the hope of

Christ. The guilt of the past is in fact over and the fear of the future is quickly replaced with the truth of God's providence. Every time we go backwards in guilt or forward in fear, we bring our minds back to the now, focus on the process of S.T.O.P. and we reframe the issue with a proper attitude. Take a deep cleansing diaphragm breath, and seek the posture of peace. We should try to breathe deeply upwards of forty times a day.

The effort at staying in the now is a major accomplishment if we can consciously do it. Worry is all about looking forward in fear. Fear then sets up catastrophic thinking and limits our minds from investigating options. Stress, fear created, is always relieved when we face the fear, erase the wrong thinking, apply faith based expectations, and replace our stress with peace!

When we are in the room, we stay in the room. We don't let our minds wander into the future. What we try to do is focus on what is going on right now in the present. Stay aware of what is going on in the moment. God has given us enough time to get everything He has planned for us to do. God has given us all the time we need. We need to work on finding and discerning His will for our plans. Live life in the moment, trusting God that He will meet your every need. It has been said by someone; Jesus gave His life for us so that He could give His life to us and live His life through us! With this in mind, fear and anxiety can be gently processed by a faith that believes we are in Christ and Christ is in us; for what, daily present victory living!

We need to ask God for wisdom for living. God is the source of all wisdom (James 1:5) and we do so need to ask, conscious and consistently ask. Actually ask for help in knowing how to handle life. Ask and you shall receive is the basis for this truth.

Learn to understand God's role in your life. He is directly involved, in even the little tiny details of your day. He is the Creator and we are the creation. He is the author of our will as reflected in our actions and our thoughts. He supplies all of my needs and in Him we are sufficient. He has set forth all the natural mechanisms of life and He is going to keep our batteries charged. We must understand our responsibility to be a doer and not just a hearer. Practice starting each day with a prayer that acknowledges God is in the day and that we are ready and willing to receive and hear His voice for wisdom. As a matter of fact, ask God to do in you this day what He has in mind! Release your will and acknowledge His perfect planned will into your "new Man".

We need to remember that prayer is not just for the foxhole. We are to seek Him in the morning and all through the day. Philippians 4:6-7 puts it this way: "Do not be anxious about anything, but in everything, by prayer and petition, with thanksgiving, present your requests to God. And the peace of God, which transcends all understanding, will guard your hearts and your minds in Christ Jesus". (NIV) We need to seek his direction in meditation and prayer, and in the practices of spiritual disciplines. Dan Wolpert reminds us that only 5% of Christians practice any form of meditation.

Joshua 1:8 tells us to meditate day and night. This practice has fallen out of favor and grace; people say it takes too much time, or is no real value. Do it anyway, practice the art, rely on it, make it a habit, and stress will go down. The world can do yoga and eat granola, why can't we learn the practice of mediation. It will help us with our problem of self-reliance. It teaches us to rest in Him where peace is really found. It is hard to worry, when worry is defined as the absence of God's provision. It is difficult when we are spending so much time concentrating on His presence, provision, and power! He is the very air we breathe. Remember, our salvation is more than an event that saved us then; but it is the reality that we are now dead to the old and raised to live in the newness of the now!

Is there a positive in stress? Yes, events of non-peace grow us in the Lord and the anchor is found again! We are yoked with the Holy Spirit and we are inexorably tied to the Lord. We are not independent agents or entities. He is so strong and capable and by the Word of the Lord we have His power. The Christian must find time for the solitude and prioritized meditation. I reenergized my prayer life by giving up some of the television and waking up earlier in the morning, before the kids start their day with Daddy this and Daddy that. What I discovered was a desire to be with Christ and not a need or must to be with Him. The Christian life is a breeze, if we can somehow just let Him do it. Practice abiding in Him, practice Getting to know Him, and practice letting Him do it...it works!

When we get overwhelmed, what is the first thing we drop? We need to acknowledge this error, own it, and take steps to rebuild our private life with God. Be aware of our spiritual gifts, and move up the ladder of dependence on Christ. There is a catch phrase shared by a friend, Mark Frueh, and he said, "Every moment of every day is about the everyday every moment Jesus!" If we give God the priority we get more done and our stress goes down. C.S. Lewis implies in his writings that when he gets overwhelmed and feels out of time, he adds another hour of prayer.

Learn to empty our psyches. Practice what I call "kinesthetic dumping". This process is designed to empty out our selectively perceived misconceptions. We are going along in our day and for no apparent or evident reason we feel sad or depressed or defeated. Our emotions have fallen prey to a thought or memory that triggers a response to life that is less than the stress free victory we want to walk in. We have two choices at this juncture, let the feeling pass and hope that it does, or attack the source and ask the Lord to clean out the old tapes and replace your thoughts with the new. We literally scan our minds for the thoughts, recognize the source as being negative and dead, cleanse the mind and tell the thoughts and tell the adversary where to go. Get in touch with what feelings you are having. This is critical to access the feelings and not just the thoughts. If we stay in our thoughts only, we ignore the enemies' best weapon…feelings!

This is a simple process of flooding; a process where we catch the critical thought and replace the negative with an affirmation or the truth as we have learned it from Christ. The old message is that you will never measure up; you are lazy. Replace that thought by cleansing the mind with the opposite positive biblical affirmations. Get up and actually move around the room and send the thoughts outside and away from you. I actually get up out of my chair and sweep, with my arms and hands, the negative thoughts outside into the street. When the thoughts try to return, I remind them that they have no power and I command them to go where they came from. My son Joseph will come out of his room, carrying his shield and his sword, and shout at the top of His voice, "I am a warrior of God and I am a child of the King". Now this is kinesthetic dumping in a dramatic way. You go Joseph!

The real issue here is that even after we have identified a hurt or a burden that we are carrying around, we still are such creatures of habit that we keep doing or allowing what we just discharged and processed by dumping to return. I am reminded of the young man who was carrying a sack full of burdens. A young pastor came along and asked him did he know he had this sack of burdens. The young man said yes, as if to be almost proud of the fact that he had these "burdens or crosses" to carry and that is what God wants him to do. The pastor reminded him that he could leave those with the Lord and pointed to a cross just a few feet away. The young man looked relieved and commenced to carry the sack over and place it at the feet of the cross. He enjoyed a glass of lemonade, refreshed him a moment, picked up the sack again and began to walk down the road carrying his sack of burdens. Why? Because we are creatures of habit, some actions are ingrained.

Sort of reminds us of Romans 7 and 8. I cannot do what I want to do, but that which I do not want to do, it is the very thing I do. Who will help cries Paul? The answer— Jesus! These are "encapsulated memories and idioms" that we need to release; and, remember, put them on a 3 x 5 card to help keep this consciously available to your mind for the opportunity for change. Practice dumping the psychic and use "kinesthetic dumping" to do so. This is a fancy created term meaning cleanse the mind with the truth of the word of God. Again, it is important to then reassess what you are feeling and take necessary action. What is needed might be a moment of praise or another movement into the direction of right thinking followed by right understanding of who you are in the new man of Christ. This is possible and I promise you, in time, your mind will catch up to the reality of what Christ has done on the cross! It is finished and the truth will and does set you free!

Stress is reduced by living life with anticipation filled with intensity, integrity, and initiative. Kristin is my six year old daughter, a lot like her older sister Beth; both intense and filled with life. When I come home she demonstrates a love of life that is all about intensity. She stands at the top of the stairs and shouts to the whole house that Daddy is home and then runs and jumps on me, almost knocking me down the stairs. You have not known intensity unless you have experienced three kids greeting mom and dad when they get home. God wants us to live with intensity; we are God's only messengers in this world.

He wants us to wake up to bless and anticipate being empowered to do the task of evangelism. Stress is always reduced when we are about the work we were designed to do. Be committed to waking up and asking God to help you fall in loved with Him newly everyday. My dear friend Evelyn says, "I may be old, but Pastor Bob, I will never be old-old!" Amen! A life of anticipation is not about being eager about what we can do, but rather, it is about being confident that in Him, the team gets it done and done well, without fear! The team, you say, is of course Christ in us!

It is a good thing to never give up and to avoid procrastination. There is a story told about a duck in North Dakota who walked up to a bar and asked the bartender if he had any raisins. The bartender said no and the duck said Ok and left. The next day the duck returned to the same bar and asked the same question about the raisins. The bartender told the duck No again and said that if he ever returned and asked again he would nail the ducks feet to the ground and tell God that he had died. The duck said OK and left. The next day, here he comes again. He stuck his head in the door, sheepishly asked the bartender if he had any nails. The bartender told him no and the duck then asked—Good! Got any raisins!

The point is to live life with intensity and then stress actually goes down because you are living alive and full of "purposeful procured integrity" and intensity; the procured part is from the Father, the purpose is ours as we bend our wills. Be honest with yourself and always honest in your dealing with others. To lack integrity is a certain and sure avenue for stress. Every time we do not say the absolute truth, we damage our self-concept and the internal stress goes up. If it didn't I would wonder if we belonged to the Lord. Take the initiative with others and with God and do without the need of return…pay forward if you please! Wake up to your purpose and love others as you strive to bless.

Be larger in your perspective; use your imagination, dream bi for God. Live life as the outpouring of the great story God has planted within you. Jeremiah 29:11 tells us God knows the plans He has for, the good and awesome plans that we can't even imagine. Live larger, not just in the hills you live on, but live to the whole world. Our perspective is so small. Satan so works to tell the Christian that the world is about "his little story" and we forget the bigger story God had planned for us. We get caught up in our stress and our own problems and we stop dreaming. Don't let the world draw you down. Never try to climb a ladder with people who are always falling off.

What all of this biblical business has been about is the focusing of our energies into becoming disciples for Christ. Our lives need to reflect the perpetual movement toward the likeness of Christ. We are after all, Christ's ones Christians. The thought here is to about knowing God by our practices of faithful discipleship; yet, at the same time, remembering that we are the finished work of Christ already. For the best reading on this concept of the new man, I refer you to the book by Dr. Steve McVey entitled *Grace Walk*. This is a definitive and readable work on the reality of who we are and whose we are and whom we work with and by!

Taking a vacation does not reduce stress, nor does going on a Bahamas cruise; this only covers or masks the under ground movements of fear, and this just for a time. Stress is prevented from becoming a problem by walking and living in the way of the cross. "I will say of the Lord, He is my refuge, my fortress, my strength, in Him will I trust". We settle for mediocrity in our faith and thusly we receive a mediocre life filled with undo unnecessary stressors. Much of what we fear never happens and yet how much anxiety did we allow!

Don't be hard on yourself. I haven't meant to put forth that image of rigidity; but it is clear to me that if stress is going to be greatly reduced and used for the growth of His children's patience, we need to work diligently at being about His business and making every effort we can to bring our lives in line with the obedience God is asking and hoping for each of us. Grace properly understood frees us from legalism. It does not however free us from the responsibility to grow in the knowledge and admonition of the Lord.

Just a few more thoughts on what we can do from the faith aspects of stress reduction. Express your faith by actions and by thoughts. Stay purposeful and meaningful, seek to set goals and answer the where questions of my life. Do the things of the Father, have moral excellence, seek the Kingdom first (Matthew

> *We settle for mediocrity in our faith and thusly we receive a mediocre life filled with undo unnecessary stressors.*

6:33-34), and put on the armor of God daily (Ephesians 6:10-17). Condition ourselves to be persons of faith by bending our wills to the Lordship of Christ; lean on Him and acknowledge Him in all that you do. Live aware of Christ through the praise of His power and through the position of like purpose. Posture your self in the pasture, resting in the words found in the 23ed Psalm. Adopt His personality and loose our own personal pattern of pious perfection. What this means is give up trying to do and measure up in our own self described religious fashions, and just be His. Obtain His image of personal excellence. In short, know Him by being responsive to Him, live in remembrance of Him, and be relaxed in Him. This is a certain and attainable mindset that puts us on the path of less stress. Now let's look at some other broader based psychological concepts for Stress Management.

C. Psychological Stress Reducers

Diet and Exercise are critical to good stress management. Exercise is the number three stress reducer, followed by laughter and crying, which I will cover in a bit. Experts all differ on the amount, but it seems the main consensus is at least three times a week for 20 minutes and this at a vigorous and aerobic heart rate. Often people will say to me I am too tired to exercise and the response I have to share is the reason they are tired is that they don't exercise. The stress buildup caused by the lack of exercise is coming out in fatigue. Exercise releases brain chemicals that relax the body and release the tension in the nervous and limbic systems. The body benefits and we feel better having been good to our bodies and ourselves.

I remember the best working program I ever had. I built a large indoor Jacuzzi and I would fill the tub up with nice hot water and relax. I would practice my relaxation skills and imagine myself exercising. I would begin to sweat, tire from the fatigue of thinking so hard, release the water from the tub and fight the current and try not to get sucked down the water pipes. This was anaerobic and aerobic exercise, all at the same time. Fantastic, Yes! This is not exactly what the sports folks have in mind, but it is creative. Another stress reducer is opening up your creativity!

As to diet, we pretty much know what is needed here, moderation with attention to types and portions of food we eat. A concept you may not be familiar with was discussed and presented in a book called *The Psycho-metabolic Blues* by Drs. Jerome and Nanette Marmorstein. This is a new and practical solution for anxiety, depression, fatigue, hypoglycemia and related stressful problems. Basically, the regimen calls for restricting sugar. As we know Americans consume more than six times more sugar than their body needs. It calls for the careful use of white refined flowers. The slogan being, the whiter the bread, the keeper you are dead. It asks that we restrict the intact of chocolate and, yes (please say it isn't true) caffeine. The authors make this statement in their book, "The long held myth that emotional health and happiness are just a matter of overcoming unhealthy attitudes and behavior, without taking into consideration the role of chemical effects on the brain and body, has impaired the efficiency of emotional therapy for years". (Page 8) I mention this concept because I have used it for over eight years and it is helpful in regulating my blood sugars and in my perceived energy levels. For sure, diet is apart of stress managing.

Another concept or skill that is easy to do is to breathe diaphragmatically. This is the process of breathing deeply upwards of forty times a day. Sit in a comfortable position; place one hand on your stomach and the other hand on your chest. Try to breathe so that only your stomach rises and falls. As you inhale, concentrate on your chest remaining relatively still while your stomach rises. It may be helpful to imagine that you have a balloon in your stomach, which you are blowing up each time you inhale. When exhaling, allow your stomach to fall in and the air to fully escape. Take deep breaths, concentrating on only moving the stomach. Hold each breath for 2-4 seconds. Do this as a pattern for your breathing for at least four times. Then return to normal breathing. It is normal for this healthy breathing to feel a little awkward at first. With practice, it will become more natural feeling.

Another breathing technique is to practice deep breathing and holding the breaths and exhaling using imagery of peace as you exhale. Breathe in deeply, hold the breath for a few seconds, and release the breath as you imagine stress and anxiety leaving your body. Make a sound with your mouth as you release the air, as the sound of wind blowing is calming. I use this all the time in conjunction with going to a quiet place in my mind. I call it accessing peace and I use it frequently to settle my mind and to refocus on truth.

Vital to stress reduction is the cultivation of support groups. I have been a part of one Bible study group for over ten years. I have been going to a Lutheran men's breakfast for over eleven years and I am not even a Lutheran. I have started a new men's group and I am looking into joining a group to help with weight management. Am I a groupie or is there something healthy in this neediness. In fact, sociologists remind us that we need more at least six support groups to make life work. We need groups that support us, challenge us, inspire us, push us to action, and just being a place to connect.

One of the worst things we can do to create stress is to isolate. One of these support groups cannot really be family. Family is vital, but the ability to be truly transparent within the family is not easy; and honestly, transparency is much of what a support system is all about. When your support group knows what is in your checkbook, it makes it harder to be open and honest. That may be why wives and husbands often have friends that they talk to more easily

> *Discernment is found in the silence of meditation and the simple asking of the Holy Spirit what is best, and turning the search over to the small still voice inside.*

than their spouse, not uncommon. The church can be one of the best support groups. Vital to stress reduction is the ability to share what you are feeling in a safe and supportive group of friends. Cultivate supports if stress reduction is your goal.

Another helpful technique useful for stress management is time management. Let go of the tyranny of the urgent. Determine of all the good what the best is. Be ready for stuff to happen. As it has been said, "stuff happens" and what you planned may not be possible; but those who handle stress best expect the unexpected. Simple rules like setting priorities, scheduling tasks for peak performance around your circadian rhythm, budget enough time to complete activities, and break up long term goals into short range goals are essential. I have discovered that I am far more productive at night than during the day, so I do much work at night (as I am right now).

Time management requires setting priorities. What can we do to determine the good from the better; again, prayer is the key. Discernment is found in the silence of meditation and the simple asking of the Holy Spirit, what is the best and turning the search over to the small still voice inside. I want to emphasize one more time; we do not allow the Holy Sprit to have enough space in our lives. We are so conditioned to solve that we find it a little uncomfortable to believe that all we really have to do is give it up to the Holy Spirit. This concept is not taught; it is just done. Once done, the results are witnessed and the practice is validated. Give it up for the Holy Spirit! Amen!

Avoid procrastination! This is the king of stress producers. In the book *Screwtape Letters*, Wormwood is instructed to not tell Christian not to do, but to do it tomorrow. It is not that life needs to be lived for the Lord, but let's get started tomorrow. Put off until tomorrow what you could have done today is a sure formula for stress. To avoid procrastination take immediate energetic applied action. Get up and do it now. As soon as you feel the urge to put something off, just get up and do it and you will immediately feel less stressed. There are many more reasons for procrastination; but for now just simply remember that if and when you get up and take action, you will feel less stressed.

You know God is going to take away our weekends if we don't change. We make the greatest to do list, make plans to get them all done on the weekend, we settle in and then before we know it, it is Sunday afternoon, and we are beating ourselves up for being lazy. If we simply would examine why we put off stuff, we will know what to ask God to help us with.

Otherwise, here comes the "tiny baseball bat". Remember, the bat is the self judgment we make about ourselves of being losers or inadequate. We are losers and the list goes on and on and on. By the way, if something is on your list for more than a week, take it off. It is not obvious very important to you and it will return to the list at another time when it is important. Trust me! This poem by Dr. Dennis Waitley is famous and so appropriate for right here.

Someday I'll

There is an Island fantasy
A "Someday I'll," we'll never see
When recession stops, inflation ceases
Our mortgage is paid, our pay increases

That someday I'll where problems end
Where every piece of mail is from a friend
Where the children are sweet and already grown
Where we all retire at forty-one

Playing backgammon in the island sun
Most unhappy people look to tomorrow
To erase this day's hardship and sorrow

They put happiness on "lay away"
And struggle through a blue today
But happiness cannot be sought
It can't be earned, it can't be bought

Life's most important revelation
Is that the journey means more than the destination
Happiness is where you are right now
Pushing a pencil or pushing a plow

Going to school or standing in line
Watching and waiting, or tasting the wine
If you live in the past you become senile
If you live in the future you're on Someday I'll

The fear of results is procrastination
The joy of today is a celebration
You can save, you can slave, trudging mile after mile
But you'll never set foot on your Someday I'll

When you've paid all your dues and put in your time
Out of nowhere comes another Mt. Everest to climb
From this day forward make it your vow
Take Someday I'll and make it yours Now!

Chapter Seven:
Be Happy! No, be content! Huh?

In this next chapter we are going to look at the process for being content. Many people wish to be happy in life and this is not all bad; however, happiness is so much tied to circumstances and issues of the day that are confronting you. Whereas, what I want for us in *Living Up In a Down World* is contentment coming from a deep joy that does not reflect circumstances but is based in the internal testimony of the truth of whose we are and to whom we serve. Joy is based in the eternal, not the temporal. To do this we are going to look at some concepts for personality focus, we are going to look at developing the important perspective of an altruistic nature; and lastly, we are going to look at the serious subject of staying humorous and having more of a childlike response to life. OK Verne, let's get it on! Even this comment ending this paragraph indicates my need to live more in touch with my childlike side of life! Christ asked to not forsake the child, but to embrace yourself in integrity; but for heaven's sake, do not avoid or deny the little you...please!

What is the difference between happiness and contentment? Webster's defines happiness simply as a state of well being, a pleasurable satisfaction. By definition then a happy person is one who has a reason to be content and is satisfied with much of what life has to offer. This happiness based in perception and influences of the moment. This perception is so controlled by externals. Contentment and happiness differ in origin and perception. Real contentment anchors in the joy of not life, but in the joy found in the deeper spiritual sense of the Word of God.

While my friend Mark was travelling In Kenya, he had the perchance to encounter a gentleman of great contentment. He noticed an elderly sheep herder attending his flock. During a conversation he had with the man, the conversation came to the thoughts of life. He elderly fellow shared with Mark that he was so glad he did not grow up in the United States. When asked why he said this, he shared that in America there were so many distractions and this he felt gave the American little chance for true contentment. For this wise older man, his contentment was not in what he had but in whose he was! This contentment expressed by the shepherd rose above circumstances and focused on the very nature and character of God. God wants his people content and happy if possible. These things I have spoken to you, that your joy may be full! (John 15:11)

In 1 Timothy 6:6-13 a great truth and syllogism for life lived up emerges. It is a super word and needs to be noted and emphasized. It says, "But godliness with contentment is great gain. It is true that we brought nothing into the world, and we can take nothing out of it. But if we have food and clothing, we will be content with that. People who want to get rich fall into temptation and a trap and into many foolish and harmful desires that plunge men into ruin and destruction. For the love of money is the root of all kinds of evil. Some people, eager for money, have wandered from the faith and pierced themselves with many grieves. But you, oh man of God, flee from all this, and pursue righteousness, godliness, faith, love, endurance and gentleness. Fight the good fight of the faith. Take hold of the eternal life to which you were called when you made your good confession in the presence of many witnesses and in the sight of God, who gives life to everything." (NIV) What a mouthful and a clear path for living up.

Great truths like this are seldom emphasized only once in the scripture, but rather is a constant theme of the writer. Paul restates this same concept in the following quote from Philippians 4:11-12., "I am not saying this because I am in need, for I have learned to be content whatever the circumstances. I know what it is to be in need, and I know what it is to have plenty. I have learned the secret of being content in any and every situation." (NIV) And then he sums it up with the quote of quotes that supplies all of our joy and contentment, because it takes the big "R" off of us (responsibility) and puts it in the Masters hands. In verse 13, God tells us through Paul, "I can do everything through him who gives me strength." (NIV) With God, it is possible! This is contentment indeed! Whoa!

Concepts for being content

1. To be content, one must know something about their "operations manual", their personality.

What do we know about our basic selves? What is our personality like under pressure? How do we perform when we are not operating in our best of spaces? What are we like when we are evidently walking around with the bag of flesh following closely behind? To be content, I feel it absolutely necessary that we understand a little about our basic personality and that we have some insights to the areas in life we need to grow and equip.

The purpose of this text, as several times earlier stated, is not to be a definitive source on any topic suggested. It is rather to cause us to search deeper if the thought attracts our interest through the Holy Sprit's gentle tweak. For our purposes here, I wish to ask you a few simple questions. These will give us the insights I am seeking to help you understand your areas of strength and weakness. This then will and does produce for us a contentment.

One of the ways that the Adversary takes our contentment is by creating in us a "doubter". This "doubter" takes any perceived area of weakness, magnifies it, and creates for us a susceptibility to the negative, and the negative prevents contentment. We are always trying to be something else, a person with no areas of weakness, because all we ever remember are these areas of weakness. If I were to ask you to list your areas of strength, you would have a very few humble responses. When asked to list your areas of weakness, the list goes on and on.

So, in an effort to soften the role of weaknesses, I affirm that we do not have areas of weakness but only areas of growth, needing to be touched by the insights of scripture. We are not "good finders" in looking at our own worth. I demonstrated this earlier in the text by the thought of the tiny baseball bat that we all carry around in our pockets.

Our minds are split, split between what it is that God is teaching and what it is that is part of our "fleshly" human experience. The flesh will always be with us. The two are always working for chairmanship of the body and the soul, the spirit is His. There is a resource and author I want to surface and acknowledge. I have greatly enjoyed the work of Gerald Jampolsky in *Love is Letting Go of Fear*. I would recommend everyone read the text, but be cautious in not approaching the text with a "new age" slant. Every concept is biblical, but it is careful to give the credit to the work of the Sprit and not to the innate goodness of man.

In his book, he says, "Our mind functions as if it were split; part of it acts as if it were directed by the ego (flesh), and the other part by love (God). Most of the time, our mind pays attention to the pseudo-director that we call our ego, which is simply another name for fear." (Page 25) He goes on to say that our minds are like the director, having the capacity to change anything about the film at anytime it wants. This is the classic illustration of the war that goes on within our minds, between good (God) and evil (ego/flesh). You can read all about this in Romans 7 and Romans 8, great read!

Let's ask a simple question and see into our basic human natures. If you were in the eighth grade and your drama teacher asked you to be in a play, what role would you like to play? Would you want to be the director, the producer, the actor, or the audience? You ask what has this to do with contentment. When we understand our natures we are more in control.

Point here, the control that we want as someone who is living up is not personal control, but relegating the control ultimately to the Spirit. What helps us is when we know ourselves we have a better avenue for making choices to

> *The control that we want as someone who is "living up" is not personal control, but relegating the control to the Holy Spirit.*

change. Change is the arena of sanctification and this is the hope of transformation, the mind of Christ in us.

Many in the field of psychology share the following understandings. Gary Smalley, Tim LaHaye, Florence Littenauer, and Aristotle among others, have all used this matrix for insights. It has been variably called DISC; Animals like lions, otters, beavers and golden retrievers; it has been called parts in a play; and been attributes of bile in the blood, like melancholic or sanguine. They all boil down to the same sense of a simple understanding of the personality and how it interacts with life. So, I give credit to them all, plus some of my own insights.

There are four concerns of this profile useful for today. What is the role you choose? What is the goal of that role? What direction or way of life does that role want? And, what does that role need to survive? These are the insights we can use to direct our path toward contentment within ourselves.

It might also be helpful to illustrate this concept through the use of Analytical and Global viewpoints on life. This might help us to extend to the other a different view if we did in fact understand it not to be personal but part of the who they are. What I am saying here is that when we understand their actions are part of who they are and are not specifically address at us; it makes a great difference in perspective. Notice the diagrams:

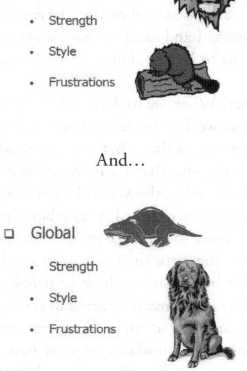

- ☐ Analytical
  - • Strength
  - • Style
  - • Frustrations

And...

- ☐ Global
  - • Strength
  - • Style
  - • Frustrations

So, here we have the concept of two overarching personality concepts. Are we global, a visionary; or are we more concrete and detailed.

So, what was your answer to the above question about the role in the play? The role of Director has as the goal to be in control; has as its direction that it must be "my way"; has as its need to being an achiever and to be appreciated for what it does, it wants to be the boss. The role of Producer has as the goal to be perfect; has as its direction that it must be the "right way"; has as its need to have things in order and have others be sensitive too its needs, cannot handle chaos. The role of Actor or Star has as the goal of life to have fun; has as its direction the happy and fun way; has as its need to seek attention, be up front, center of things and to find acceptance and approval. Lastly, the role of audience member has as its goal to have peace; has as its direction the easy way; has as its need to be respected and needs to have others stroke its low self worth, wants to be left alone and wishes to watch from the sidelines.

So now what? When we understand these basic thoughts about ourselves, we can be less crucial and condemning; especially when we realize that we are products of our collective histories, and that what we are can be changed. We can become more like the Master by learning to blend and adapt our strengths of personality, grabbing from the good and learning to grow the areas of growth that show up.

For example, the actor or star is so in need of attention that they might be seen as shallow or people pleasers. No backbone and no real sense of leadership skills. The director is so bossy and arrogant at times, as to seen inflexible and a very poor listener. The producer so must have it their way, or it's the highway for dissenters. No tolerance for others thought and opinions. There is absolutely a right way. And the audience member is seen as timid and a wallflower, no hope here. When we know that this is the way the world has "bent" us, we can seek change and ask the Holy Sprit for help in becoming tempered in who we are and to manifest more of the "redeemed' qualities found in spirit control.

For example, every one follows a leader with confidence, but it's more easily done when the confident one has a heart changed and is a redeemed leader. When the leader is following the basic natures of the flesh, he or she can appear harsh and unrelenting in getting the job done at almost any cost. The matter of the heart being broken creates the change necessary for contentment to be true; otherwise, our unknown areas of growth and our overly passionate egos always bumps into the psyche, causes incongruence and personal feelings of inadequacy and dissent feeds the split I mentioned earlier.

For much more on this personality insight, I refer you to the above authors listed in the early paragraphs. It is fascinating journey, especially as we learn about our darker selves and submit these traits to the control of the Spirit. When we do this, we become more like Jesus who had all four personalities operating at one and the same time, using the strengths he needed, accessed from each personality as the situation dictated. Yes!

2. Five attributes of contentment as discovered in a survey.

I enjoyed the work of John Stossel, an investigative reporter on the networks. He did a study asking Americans what it took for them to be happy. He did not use the word content, but it is close enough. He found that the happiest people had these five attributes in their lives and they asked themselves these questions. Was their life purposeful and meaningful? Was their life connected to multiple relationships of support? Did they feel they were in control? Were they an optimistic people? And, did they develop their own sense of personal faith? I felt these each could be apart of answering for us the way to the goal of contentment.

Stay purposeful and meaningful in your life is what? Is it in finding your ministry? Is it feeling useful and not just here and not alive? Isn't it what all of us who are aging fear the most? Yes to these all. The need to be meaningful and purposeful is critical. Many people feel that we have enough money, or if we are successful enough in life, or if we are popular or influential, life will be good. This is just not deep enough; all these are shallow. The real need in life is to feel as if what you are doing has impacted life and that you have made a difference. Will what I have done and is what I am doing making a difference in my life or in anyone else's? We need to feel significant and valued. We need to feel authentic, useful, and empowered in being of value and worth in the world we live in.

This is why our faith is so important, because God is the author of our purposes. In Him we have purpose. We need to wake each day asking that God would bless not what we are doing, but to help us make sure what we are doing He is in! Join in where God is already working. Don't ask God to bless your work, but to rather ask God to bless us in the work of where He is already working. In other words, join God in His work and ask for discernment to know where He is going. Wow! Lord, help us to join in to what you are doing in our world. We want to be a part of the power of your presence in this world. Lord, join me to you as we do! We need to feel purposeful and that what we are doing has meaning. In Christ it is and does!

The survey also suggested the need to be apart of something bigger than we are and to feel connected to lots of supports. This is the concept of not going it alone. Contentment is definitely found in being a part of a team. Team means together we accomplish more! Did you ever notice geese flying overhead? This is very common in North Dakota. They fly in a "V" formation. Why? Because they know that in flying this way, they can fly 63% further than if they flew in singular fashion. How do they know this? It is that God made them to know. God gave everything a purpose, and the very D.N.A. of these geese knows to fly this way. We must also fly together.

God made us this way. We are not made for isolation. God made us in His image and He chooses to make us for His companionship.

Thirdly, another aspect of this survey was to feel in control. In the study, Ted pointed out that this meant, did we feel a sense in which we knew about our futures, that we knew about where our next meal was coming from, that we knew that we had food and shelter and health? It meant, did we know that our nation was secure and did our jobs have longevity, would we be employed tomorrow? These were all externals and greatly dependent on government and such. The parallel for the

> *Our security and control is based in our faith and the solidness of the message of the cross. Our hope is built on nothing less than Jesus Christ and His righteousness.*

Christian is that we do not need to feel in control, God is. His providential care is secure and his purposes for us are certain. We can live in the "certainties of the Spirit" and not in our own self created certainties, which are always subject to external pressures and doubts. Our security and control is based in our faith and the solidness of the message of the cross. Our hope is built on nothing less than Jesus Christ and His righteousness...and that is enough!

Fourthly, the survey listed the idea of practicing optimism. This is the ability to see the best in all circumstances. It is the want to seek out first the good we see and then to suggest what might need change only after we compliment. Here we ask how much of our Eior shows up each day. This is the little donkey that is so pessimistic and looks always for the worst. Where is our attitude of gratitude and attitude of altitude? To be optimistic is not to be foolish hearted, but it is to believe in the overall direction that God has for your life is good. Romans 8:28 teaches us that all things work together for the good according to his purposes for those who are called of Him. This optimism is not founded on pie in the sky, but on Calvary and the promises of God. This definitely brings contentment and joy!

The fifth element listed was developing your faith. I found it curious that in a secular study this element of contentment was one of the key five. The people, by the way, found to be happiest were the Amish people; primarily because their simplicity of life and their strong faith formation. When we develop our faith, we are placing hope and validation outside of our own control. We are gaining an external source of worth and wisdom, which has as its affect to help us stop rejecting ourselves and helps us to stop always looking for our shortcomings. There is so much implied in this fifth thought, but for now it is my prayer that for each of you who are reading this text, that you will develop your personal faith, become a disciple, and walk in His strength. I hope that your faith will serve as healer for your wounds and will give you the proper value and esteem your Creator intended. So much more!

3. Be aware of your "being" and your" doing" and focus Up and Out, and not Down and In.

Be an artist, not a performer. An artist knows who he is, he is what he is, and it is all he can be. A performer is more about what he does, how he makes a living, and it is not just an occupation and not the essence of his being. When we live conscious of our being and not our doing, it places the crux of the power in God's hands and not in ours, which can fail and crumble easily. Contentment is about peace and peace is about no worries, because worries are God's job. Tied to this is the need and attribute of focusing up and not down, out and not in. We look up for the empowerment and out for the mission and ministry and purpose God gives us for this creation. . When we focus in we focus on self and our power and when we look down we turn from the source and find depression and sadness. Contentment is found in the presentation of being up and out in a down and in world! We must be a people of external focus and not be strong about "navel gazing" and promoting our own good to the exclusion of others. Greater love has no man than he lay down his life for others, even a friend!

4. To be content we must constantly monitor our attitude.

I know that we have stated this before, but the repetition here I feel is needed and significant. I want to share this point around a cute story I picked up along the way, it is called simply Attitude is. The story is about a 92-year-old, petite, well poised and proud lady, who is

> *We wake up each day like chickens, in a new world; we realize the grace given and the gift given by the Creator, no concerns for food or such, just gratitude for being alive and being blessed.*

fully dressed each morning by eight o'clock, with her hair fashionably combed and makeup perfectly applied; even though she is legally blind, moves to a nursing home today. Her husband of 70 years recently passed away, making the move necessary.

After many hours of waiting patiently in the lobby of the nursing home, she smiled sweetly when told her room was ready. As she maneuvered her walker to the elevator, the attendant or aide provided a visual description of her tiny room, including the eyelet sheets that had been hung on her window. "I love it", she stated with the enthusiasm of an eight-year-old having just been presented with a new puppy. "Mrs. Jones, you haven't seen the room, just wait." "That doesn't have anything to do with it", she replied. "Happiness is something you decide on ahead of time. Whether I like my room or not doesn't depend on how the furniture is arranged, it's how I arranged my mind; I have already decided to like it."

She went on, as the attendant, captured by her wisdom listened. "It's a decision I make every morning when I wake up. I have a choice; I can spend the day in bed recounting the difficulty I have with the parts of my body that no longer work, or get out of bed and be thankful for the ones that do. Each day is a gift, and as long as my eyes open, I'll focus on the new day and all the happy memories I've stored away just for this time of my life. Old age is like a bank account; you withdraw from what you've put in. So, my advice to you would be to deposit a lot of happiness in the bank account or memories. Thank you for your part in filling my bank account. I am still depositing."

How very, very true this is! We wake up each day like chickens, in a new world; we realize the grace given and the gift given by the Creator, no concerns for food or such, just gratitude for being alive and blessed. Yeah chickens; learned this in Kenya! Chickens are the Kenyans best friends. You feed it; it takes care of itself, stays loyal, and gives you a gift everyday...an egg! You tie its legs; throw it in the back of a truck. It wakes up in darkness and still lays an egg. It belongs to the yard and it knows its mission and purpose…lay an egg! Go chickens and go Kenya!

This reminds me of a dear friend in Minot that always says, "I may be old, but I will never be old-old!" Our attitudes are attitudes of gratitude and always thankful for the beauty of each day God gives, looking to make the best and to see the best, in our world, and in the worlds of others. Thanks again Evelyn! I needed that! She is a friend whose contentment is in her attitude of altitude!

5. To be content we must develop a sense of Altruism.

Altruism is the giving of one self to others without the sense of any direct return. No greater gift do we have than the ability to give ourselves away. Remember, that all that we give we get back in return. This is the principle that teaches that every gift of a smile, a gesture, assistance with some type of financial aid, any "intentional act of kindness", is returned to us from within. The Sprit so honors the honest and gracious gift and the result is a peaceful presence. The Bible teaches that we shall know them by their love. I then define love as the extension of oneself to another so that the other might become more of God intended them to be. In other words, it is the extension of oneself to the betterment and hope for growth of the other. So, I believe contentment is found or at least prospered when we give ourselves away in an altruistic fashion. It is the catchword I coined and have used all the book of "Intend to Extend". I also have called it being a "good finder".

Let's acknowledge for a second that each of these terms have and can be found in secular and non-religious books.

I shared this with you when I mentioned the book; *Love is letting go of Fear*, by Gerald Jampolsky. His book does not mention Christ, as a matter of fact, he is careful not to. It was written in the seventies and the popular notion then was to refer to God in the aphorism of LOVE. Everything was love. Again this is to me an effort to go around the reality that we are not in control and it is not all about us, but it is all about God. Nevertheless, here is my point. The thoughts of this book were very impressing on me, I still find myself rereading some portions of the text, being very careful to make sure I infuse and inject the content with the truth of God's word. This is for some troublesome and they refer to it as "psychobabble". Not so! This very idea of being a good finder and intending to extend are concepts that are all very deeply biblical. The truths of God's word are universal, but the belief in the risen and crucified Christ is Christian. The point is to take from literature and writings truth, extract them, and give them the support and truth of God's word. How do I mean? Even in these thoughts what occurs to me is the define principle of forgiveness as being an ultimate way of giving oneself away.

To be altruistic is to be forgiving and extending of your need to be right and to, in fact, give up the need to counterattack. A counterattack is a verbal device that protects us from being wrong or of being hurt. It projects in anger and has as its base fear. Fear of rejection or fear of being shamed, are all very common to our childhoods. So, when we give up our need to protect, we in essence, forgive. Forgiveness is the key to inner peace. Inner peace cannot be found without the practice of forgiveness, forgive others lest you not be forgiven. Do I dare tell another joke? Ya sure, go ahead!

Ole and Lena were sitting in their cabin one cold winter day and Ole was feeling the old "cabin fever". So he turned to Lean and told her he wanted to go down to the K Mart and buy a puzzle. So they got in the car and headed down to the store and when they got there, Ole looked over all the puzzles, and he picked one he knew was going to be a keeper. It was a beautiful picture and it was a massive one hundred-piece puzzle. He bought it and took it home and put it on the green card table, you know the table where you always do puzzles. After a while, he and Lena got her down and they were happy about the way it turned out. They decided to glue it and put it on the wall. It was keeper after all, "dontcha know." About that time Lars, Ole's friend called and asked how he was doing. Ole told him about the puzzle and Lars asked him was it a good one? Ole said it was a keeper and they were going to put it on the wall. Lars said that was good and then asked Ole how long it took them to do the puzzle. Ole said about ten to twelve hours. Lars asked was that good and Ole told, "Sure it is. It says four to six years on the box!" Now that is a friend and someone who understood being a good finder! He could have easily told Ole that was the age recommend for buying, not getting the puzzle done.

Being altruistic also involves being a good listener. Listening takes time and time is a gift not so easily given. What many people need, and what in turn so feeds your sense of peace, is for someone to just listen to them for a while. As a pastoral counselor I often will just be a good listener. Carl Rogers, one of the early fathers of psychotherapy, had a technique of listening that he called "unconditional positive regard". He would just listen and mutter and then asked you to tell him what you had figured out the answer to be. Genius!

The story is told that a young man took an ad out in the LA times and stated that he would listen to you, uninterrupted for thirty minutes, for only five dollars. He made a living. Remember, when you are listening, listen and be careful when you do speak not to say "I agree, but". Rather I would have you say "I agree, and". The ",but" says I really don't agree and people will become defended when your goal was to just let them share, only to quickly offer your counter thought. Listening altruistically is a part of contentment; trust me!

> Contentment is gained when we freely give ourselves away. All that we give we get in return. Jampolsky was right on this!

6. Develop a good sense of humor and contentment is apart of the gains!

Stress relief leads to contentment and laughter and crying are the two top stress relievers, which it makes sense would lead to content and settled spirit. I earlier said to learn to "jest for the fun of it". Children laugh upwards of four hundred times a day; adults laugh less than eight. Why? We adults are suffering from "HDS/TS" or in non-technical terms, humor deficiency syndrome/terminal seriousness. We do not look for humor in our everyday lives. Humor releases all kinds of happy hormones in the brain. It is a proven fact of science that laughter is calming. The Bible extols us to have a happy heart. So laugh, lighten up and look for the humor in things.

This is not a natural occurrence for many of us, so you may have to work at it a bit. And then again, for some of us we need to be more serious. You can't win for losing; all you can do is try. I could say so much more, but the thought is rather self evident and I just wanted to "lighten you up" to the idea of humor. What kind of lights did Noah have on the Ark? Pause...floodlights! Or even better, what kind of lights did Moses have on the Ark...None, not Moses! Go ahead, let loose, and laugh! Ok, don't scrooge!

Dr. Colbert in his work titled, *Stressless*, believes strongly in the ability for laughter to create the atmosphere needed for contentment. He says that laughter is innate, a part of our making; and laughter is contagious, a love giving tonic for others. He says to make laughter and happiness a habit.

One final thought here, happiness and contentment are not synonymous but related. Contentment certainly contains happiness, but happiness does not necessarily lead to contentment. There is an emerging science out there that is concerning itself with the study of happiness. Now I contend that happiness is a subset of contentment and that our faith produces a contentment that the world cannot fathom. So, I make this thought available for your pondering. There is a deep human need for spirituality and meaning, and the psychology of happiness is helping modern researchers take afresh look at faith issues. Isn't it amazing, all thought seems to evolve or rotate eventually back to the deep hole in our hearts that only God can fill. God made us to need him and that is what it is all about...contentment included!

Chapter Eight:
Wrap up/Recap and Final Thoughts: A Look at the Philosophy of Being Up

So here we are, at the beginning of the end of this journey. It is an end, which only begins, with where you go with these thoughts for yourself. Certainly, I can hope that you will think about what has been said, ponder and question if it fits for you. What I hope for you is that you have seen that the peace that is promised in scripture is possible. God made us to live up in a down world. He made us to be dependent on Him for our very essence of self. When we stray away and become more and more self-reliant, no peace and no upward living is possible. I hope you will go back now and read and reread some sections of the text and ask yourself how am I applying any of this to my life? God help me to be open enough to the truths that are here and to incorporate them into my life. Show me Father what is for me and what is for another. What have I learned and what is it that I can share with someone to whom I might meet or share a journey with.

I ask that you make a choice to make a difference. Set you wills to excellence and let your wills be bent to the desire of the Father. Bend your wills to your gifts. Discover the gifts that God has given you. Use them in your ministry of being a "good finder". Ask God to show you your ministry and be about reaching out and intending to extend to others. Seek peace and give up the need to attack others, it only ends up minimizing your worth and drains your energy.

Don't go it alone. Take to heart the scripture that enjoins us to not forsake the gathering of the saints. God's church is not in trouble, never has been and never will be. We are certainly in an era of metamorphosis, maybe even a post Christian age, but we must not isolate and draw back into our self conceived visions of personally created self reliant kingdoms. I am suggesting that we pursue a fellowship that feeds our spirits and connects us to the body to receive the benefits of body life; the need for connectedness and validation and support, in an authentic, credible and familial setting. Be like the gees and fly further with each other's help. I sincerely believe that the loss of the church's role as connector is one of the Adversary greatest historical schemes. He is always done it and he is doing it again by telling us we don't need the church, it is just a building. But it this building where God's people meet to know and to grow in what makes a difference... personal faith in Christ, the revealed truth of God.

Know you are a winner! Be conditioned for success! Communicate from an empowerment in the knowledge of knowing who and whose you are. It is in our being and not in our doing that we fins the strength to be up in a down world. This seems so evident, but our world does not promote being, it promotes doing. We are measured by our doings and not our beings. Learn to answer the question of how are you doing by saying "I am being fine!" Communicate with the idea of gifting and blessing the other person. Always talk with the person and not to or at the person. Talk from a space of equality and not as one who has the answers but as one gently seeking the answers also. God creates winners. Ask the Lord to affirm this in your life. Lord, if you are not there, don't send me! In other words, Lord help me to join in with what you are already doing in our world. I will succeed and have succeeded based on "Your" involvement. Lord be in what you have me doing. Help me to be "Your winner"

Ask God to change you. See tribulation as an opportunity for gaining insight to ourselves, so that we might make personally empowered choices for change. Remember, peace comes through the deep understanding that God has overcome the world and we are His adopted and chosen children. God please mature me! This needs to be the cry of every upward traveler. Realize the cost if you don't grow and adapt and be open to new thoughts and concepts. Invest in growth. Study and look into the Word of God, join study groups, spend time reading and praying, fasting if need be. Research books on the devotional life, such as Dan Wolpert's, *Creating a Life with God*. Invest in your finances, but much more needed is the investment of your life into Christ.

Remember, it is a process. It is the process of sanctification, which we have eluded to earlier many times. This sanctification is already real in the new man. Our mission is to live to the reality of the mew man and to bring our relationships to Christ as the forefront of our mindsets. It is not a "one two three" program of change, but a daily learning that rewards in great benefits of peace and contentment and a life of living up. The self help process is a part of the overall process. Be gently with yourself. It takes time, but the growth process is so much fun when you realize that God is in it and He has already given you the trophy...salvation and permanence in His kingdom. I am not sure of the origin of this poem, but it has meant a lot to me and I want to share it with you. Read it slowly and don't get ahead. It is called:

Autobiography in Five Short Chapters

[1]
I walk, down the street. There is a deep hole in the sidewalk.
I fall in. I am lost...I am hopeless. It isn't my fault. It takes forever to find a way out.

[2]

I walk down the same street. There is a deep hole in the sidewalk. I pretend I don't see it. I fall in again. I can't believe I am in the same place. But, it isn't my fault. It stills takes a long time to get out.

[3]

I walk down the same street. There is a deep hole in the sidewalk. I see it is there.
I still fall in...it's a habit. My eyes are open. I know where I am.
It is my fault. I get out immediately.

[4]

I walk down the same street. There is a deep hole in the sidewalk.
I walk around it!

[5]

I walk down another street!

. . . .

By Portia Nelson

This poem is so true and has captured my philosophy of living up. We are walking down a street, it is our choices that determine to a large extent how life goes, it is not anyone else's fault, we have learned to stop blaming and take personally responsibility, turn it over to God, and walk down His another street! Amen and Amen!

Let us together say good-bye for now by the sharing of two stories that have meant the entire world to me. I first remember sharing these at Abita Springs First Baptist church. Thanks to those fine folks who allowed me to join them on our journeys.

We all know the famous practice of escaping. It is said that a great escape artist was challenged to escape from a prison cell in England that no one had ever escaped from. The media was present, the papers were there, and this artist walked into the cell self-confident that he could escape. As soon as the guard left, the artist reached inside his belt and retrieved a piece of wire that he placed there earlier. Using the wire, he fashioned a simulated key, and then began to use it to open the locked door. After several attempts, frustrated and sweating, he fell exhausted into the door. The door swung open. Much to his amazement, this escape artist was trying to unlock an unlocked door. You see, the artist's confidence was the downfall of his success. The artist was so confident in his ability that he did not consider the obvious. The artist launched out on their own confidence and failed due to a misplaced confidence. The point I drew from this story is that we must fall into the hands of our own self-confidence. We were made to rely on the Sprit and learn to adapt and grow; otherwise, we too shall try to unlock an already unlocked door. The path has been shown, the provision has been made, and the peace is assured, only when we let Him pay the price and take ourselves into the learner's mode; a learner for Christ, living up in a down world being our goal by the grace and awesomeness of God. We can't but He has!

Ted Stossel at ABC News has summed it up this way! I alluded to this earlier, here reemphasized for sake of critical recap!

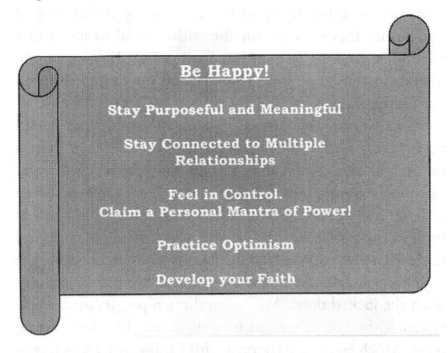

Be Happy!

Stay Purposeful and Meaningful

Stay Connected to Multiple Relationships

Feel in Control.
Claim a Personal Mantra of Power!

Practice Optimism

Develop your Faith

A final story, at least finally for now and in this book. I feel we shall journey together again. It is told to me that a famous writer traveled through North Dakota. I enjoy this story so because I now live and breathe deep clean air in the Dakota vastness. A great vastness it is indeed, on with the story. He wrote of the state that he did not enjoy it very much because he woke to candlelight and went to bed by the very same light. He noticed our long and dark winters. One night he asked his Nanny to come upstairs and look out of the window and see what he was looking at. When the Nanny arrived, this particular author asked her what she saw. She replied that she saw the lamplighter lighting the lamp posts like she had every day of her life.

The author asked her to look again and she said once more she saw a lamplighter doing his job. The young man sighed, looked at the lamppost and said this to his nanny, "Nanny, you don't see it do you? It is not just a lamplighter lighting the lamposts at night, it is a man making holes in the darkness so that others can see!" This is what I have walked by. I pray for you that you will go forward in your journey with Christ, grow and ask to change, remembering that we are all here to "make holes in the darkness so that others might see!"

Remember this please...

"The selfsame wind that blows one ship to Heaven blows another to Hell; it is not the force of the gale that determines the course, but rather the set of the sail!"

Be about setting your sails for His excellence and Live up in a down World. Shalom! Thanks Colonel Sessions, for the memory! And thanks to Colonel and Mrs. Robert B. Edwards Sr. to whom this book is dedicated and conceived! And thanks to Bogey for her help.

Author's Epilogue

So where do we go from here and to some degree where have we been! These concepts were learned in the school of hard knocks, anchored in the understanding that God uses and sees tribulation as a means to personal growth and maturity in Christ. The idea all through the book is the thought that in the transformation of our thinking and in the recognition of who we really are, we find meaning, purpose, and mostly Peace! These thoughts are anchored in the idea of seeing life through "Eternal eyes". Using these eyes we can learn to go vertical and relate our lives to the way of the Master.

The basic concepts of *Living Up In A Down World* will soon be incorporated into a trilogy, or possible more, of books speaking to specific issues that we as committed Christians often suffer from. For example, a book on marriage and a book on depression! I hope that these will also bless and encourage the body of Christ!

I have enjoyed the journey and it is my prayer that we together have had fun! So, what did the mother buffalo say to the baby buffalo when she first left him at school? Are you ready? BISON!